CW00539370

JERSEY JAUNTS

Front cover:Walkers on the coast path above Bouley Bay.
Photograph courtesy Chris Stubbs, Channel Island Publishing

JERSEY
JAUNTS

36 Short(ish) Circular Walks

John Le Dain
(author of 'Jersey Rambles')

SEAFLOWER BOOKS

First published in 2007
Revised, expanded and reprinted in 2010 by
SEAFLOWER BOOKS
16A St John's Road
St Helier
Jersey   JE2 3LD

www.ex-librisbooks.co.uk

Origination by Seaflower Books

Printed by Cromwell Press Group
Trowbridge, Wiltshire

ISBN 978-1-903341-41-4

~
To Bella & Poppy,
my Jersey granddaughters,
may they enjoy walking their Island
~

Key to CONTENTS opposite:

Easy walk; no steep slopes

Moderate effort required; some climbing

Guaranteed to make you puff!

CONTENTS

INTRODUCTION

My book *Jersey Rambles* first appeared in 1992. Just one of the walks from early editions of *Jersey Rambles* is included in the present book but rest assured that this new book contains 36 walks, none of which appears in the current edition of *Jersey Rambles*.

The number of rights of way in the Island which are off-road is slowly being added to but it is a fact that the extent of metalled lanes far exceeds that of paths and unmade tracks. Nevertheless, such lanes generally make for pleasant, pedestrian-friendly walking, particularly those designated Green Lanes, where priority is given to pedestrians, cyclists and horse riders and motor traffic is restricted to a speed limit of 15mph. Such lanes generally do not provide through-routes for motor vehicles but serve only the dwellings reached by them, so remain relatively quiet. I tried hard in compiling *Jersey Jaunts* to avoid walking on A-, B- and C-roads and to exploit, as fully as possible, opportunities to walk either off-road or via unclassified and Green Lanes. However, in certain cases it has proved impossible to devise a circular walk which avoids negotiating a busy, pavementless road for an uncomfortable distance.

A café or pub is usually to be found at the starting/finishing points of the walks so that you can choose whether to indulge and then walk it off or whether to complete the walk as a means of sharpening your appetite! Alternatively, there are usually good spots to enjoy a picnic en route.

I have known Jersey all my life but only came here to live in 2005 since when I have enjoyed far greater opportunity to explore the island's byways. Since 1992, when I published *Jersey Rambles*, trends which were underway then have largely continued. The island's population is still rising and, with it, the inevitable pressure on land, roads and infrastructure. Nevertheless, for the most part Jersey manages to cope with this pressure remarkably well.

There remains a surprising amount of unspoilt countryside. Some farmland is reverting to the wild. But even wild land needs to be managed and this is being done to advantage. The concentration of new housing development in St Helier and the parish centres is a sound policy which relieves pressure on the countryside. Much recent new building is attractive though there are some truly dreadful exceptions. I won't mention my personal *bêtes noirs* because they are quite likely to be someone else's favourites, not to mention their personal home.

Many people in Jersey, as in England, bemoan the demise of agriculture. It is true that one no longer so frequently sees Jersey cows. The island herd is concentrated into a few large units. Where once one would find cows tethered in a field or at the roadside to make the most of a few square metres of grazing one will now not see a cow for miles but then happen upon a large field full of them.

Yet agriculture is far from moribund. One of the delights of island life is having access to a wide range of vegetables, fruit and herbs which are Jersey-grown so are likely to be fresh and will not have travelled more than a few miles from where they grew. And we enjoy Jersey Dairy's excellent range of products; not just milk and cream but superb yogurt, crème fraiche and ice cream.

Many former farmhouses and their outbuildings have been redeveloped to provide several living units and sold on to folk working in the finance or legal industry. The scrubbed up appearance of such sites, particularly the former farmyards, perhaps once the domain of hens and farm cats, contrasts with a preference for car parking space. And the vegetable patch close to the house is now likely to provide a manicured environment of perfect grass and specimen trees and shrubs. Not altogether unattractive maybe, but certainly a change in character from how it used to be. Nevertheless, it is surely preferable to recycle such old properties than to demolish and build anew, as is usually the case in St Helier.

There appear to be more trees in the Island today than formerly, thanks to landowners and the good work of the Jersey branch of Men of the Trees, now known as the less gender-specific Trees for Life. 1991, when I first researched the walks for *Jersey Rambles*, was only a few years after the devastation caused by the Great Hurricane of 1987 with the loss of so many trees. Since then there has been a concerted effort to replant and the island today appears to be more thickly covered with trees than for many years.

One startling change since I first published *Jersey Rambles* is the decline of tourism, most noticeably the disappearance of hotels and guest houses; indeed, the number of beds has more than halved in that time. Hotels have been redeveloped as apartments or nursing homes. Fewer visitors mean reduced demand for the sorts of attractions which were once offered with visitors in mind. At the same time it is probably true that the modern visitor is more discerning than his or her predecessor and that the quality of visitor attractions has much improved. More and more tourists come to Jersey to enjoy the natural beauty of the island and walking is certainly the finest way to appreciate it.

I am prejudiced, of course, but to my mind Jersey remains a most attractive and alluring place. The fact of its being a small island, with the sea never far away, lends it a special magic. The coast is extraordinarily varied, with its mix of long sandy beaches, small coves and rugged headlands. The island may not possess what could precisely be called hills but its elevated surface is scored with dozens of valleys so that ways inland are seldom on the level but always rising and falling, usually gently but sometimes quite steeply. These valleys always carry a stream and their often steep sides are generally well wooded. The interior of the island is therefore characterised by a host of little valleys, each with its particular personality.

I trust that the routes in *Jersey Jaunts* will help you discover more of the joys that Jersey offers those on foot.

Each of the sketch maps in this book is accompanied by a small picture of a detail seen en route. If you keep your eyes open you should be able to spot their whereabouts. Some are easier to find than others – they are not always in front of you so you may have to look around to locate them.

J Le D, Jersey, April 2007

NOTE ON THE SECOND EDITION

During January and February 2010, I rewalked all of the 33 routes which appeared in the first edition of *Jersey Jaunts*, and very much enjoyed doing so, despite the unusually cold conditions. Some updating was clearly required – particularly with regard to pubs and hotels, some of which had either disappeared or been renamed. No sooner had the 2007 edition been published than the place of refreshment referred to in the first route around Vallée des Vaux – the Harvest Barn – closed!

For this revised edition, I have added three new routes, bringing the total to 36. Happy jaunting!

J Le D, Jersey, May 2010

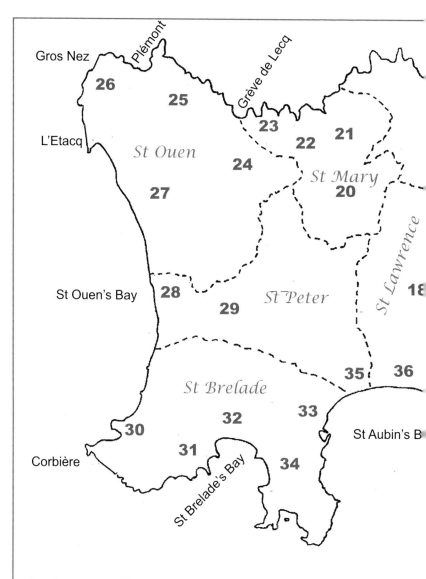

Outline map of Jersey, showing the twelve parishes and the main points around the coast.
The numbers refer to the approximate whereabouts of each of the 36 walks described in this book

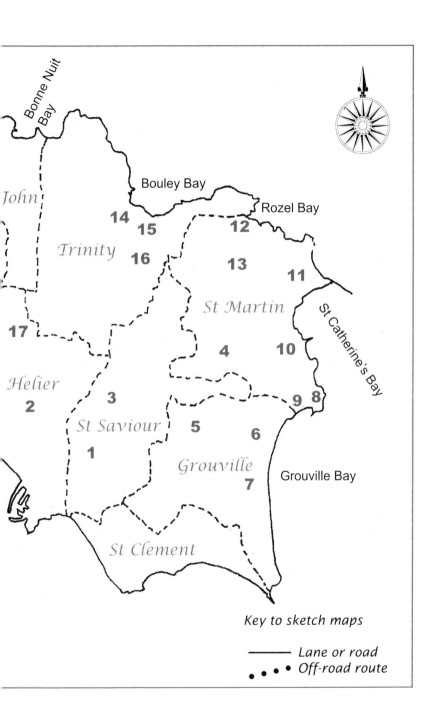

Bonne Nuit Bay

John

Trinity

Bouley Bay

Rozel Bay

14
15
16

12
13
11

St Martin

St Catherine's Bay

17

Helier

2

4
10

3

St Saviour

9 **8**

1

5
6

Grouville

7

Grouville Bay

St Clement

Key to sketch maps

——— Lane or road
•••• Off-road route

1 SWISS VALLEY
via Les Varines and Longueville Manor

This short walk explores Swiss Valley – a traditional beauty spot not far from St Helier. Unfortunately, there is an unavoidable stretch along the busy Longueville Road.

Distance:	2.5 kilometres
Getting there:	Bus route No. 1b, 2c, 22
Parking:	There is a small car park, by permission of the land-owner, in the corner of a field near the junction of Les Varines and Rue du Beauvoir. This is signposted Le Val Aume, Footpath. If arriving from town by bus alight at Longueville Manor and start the walk from there – point **A** on sketch map.
Refreshment:	None

- To begin the walk: To save the footpath through Swiss Valley until the end of the route, start by crossing the road, **Les Varines**, in front of **Millemont House**, to reach the narrow path which runs parallel to the road and make a gentle descent. There are good views across the valley to the built-up edge of town, including Jersey College for Girls and out to sea.

- Carry on until the path ends, then turn right to descend further, via **Ivystill Lane**. At the foot of the lane you reach the contemporary dwelling on the right. Here you turn left to follow the unmade track. Negotiate the 6-bar gate ahead, between old farm buildings to follow the road beside a row of semi-detached houses on your left.

- At the main road turn left and follow Longueville Road , past the foot of **Les Varines**, then **Brickfield Lane**, until you pass in front of **Longueville Manor**, one of the Island's most prestigious hotels and restaurants. (This stretch along Longueville Road is short on charm and rural peace but can be covered in not much more than five minutes.)

- Immediately past Longueville Manor, turn left into **Rue St Thomas**. You will now quickly enter Jersey's rural hinterland. Pass the turning to the left - Rue de la Freminerie - and that on the right - Rue Messervy, where the pavement runs out. Look out for the next turning on the left - **Route des Champs** - and head up here.

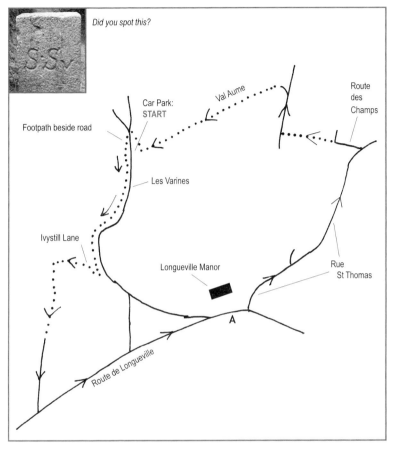

Did you spot this?

Car Park: START

Footpath beside road

Val Aume

Route des Champs

Les Varines

Ivystill Lane

Longueville Manor

Rue St Thomas

A

Route de Longueville

The lane soon bends to the right – here look out for a track straight ahead, between **Rose Cottage** on the left and an ivy hedge on the right. The path climbs gradually to reach the lane, Rue de la Freminerie. Here turn right. Very soon you reach a fork – take the left fork signposted **Le Val Aume: Footpath**. Now you begin the descent of Swiss Valley. The path goes through a pair of granite posts.

At the foot of the valley you can look left along a grassy meadow between wooded slopes which reaches down to Longueville Manor. The stream is dammed to your right to form a pond.

Now carry on uphill to ascend the slope back to the car park where, if you arrived by car, you began the walk.

2 VALLÉE DES VAUX
via Grande Route du Mont à l'Abbé

This is an interesting walk around one of the Island's rather hidden and seldom visited valleys. Buses do not venture here. The start and finish point at B&Q is not the most alluring but much of the walk is off-road along wooded hillsides.

Distance:	3 kilometres	
Getting there:	Bus route No. 5, 19	
Parking:	No public car parks; limited on-road parking	
Refreshment:	None	

To begin the walk: With your back to B&Q turn left and soon take the first turning left. At the T-junction ahead you exit **Rue des Canons** and turn right. This is **Grande Route du Mont à l'Abbé**, a designated Green Lane.

Carry on until you reach **Ruelle de Rauvet** where you turn right. Cross **St John's Road**, with care, bear left and follow the pavement to reach the next lane on the right – **Rue des Côtils**, which you turn into. This way is straight at first, then, at Les Côtils Farm, begins to twist and turn as it descends to the valley.

At the foot of this lane, turn right down Vallée des Vaux to reach the former **Harvest Barn**, once a watermill, then a pub and now the Jersey Dental Technology Centre. At the end of the car park turn left up the lane, **Route du Petit Clos**, indicated NO ENTRY. After no more than a hundred metres, look out for the entrance to a footpath through the woods on your right. Follow this way above the sunken lane on your left. Soon the path bears to the right, away from the lane.

You reach a stone wall on your left. Follow this wall which marks a field boundary. The path forks: take the left fork to follow the way beside the wall and enjoy the views across the treetops in the valley. Eventually it begins to descend, then doubles back on itself a little way up-valley before dropping you onto the road.

Turn left and look out for a formidable granite staircase on your right, beside the hillside signposted **La Fiotterie**, which leads up from the road on the far side – this will be your way back up from the valley to Grande Route du Mont à l'Abbé, but first we may explore a little more of Vallée des Vaux.

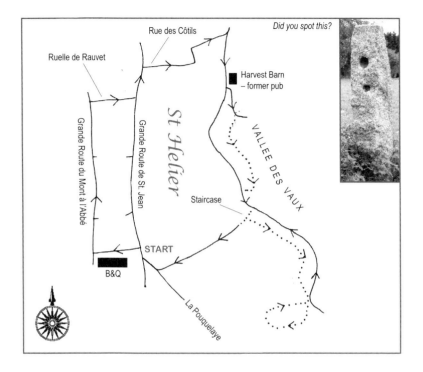

Climb five flights (42 steps) of the granite staircase opposite. Now bear left along the hillside path. Follow this undulating path until you reach a wider cross-track leading up from the road below.

Cross this former drive to follow the hillside path in the same direction. This will eventually lead you back down to the road beside the house named **Le Jardin de la Fontaine**. You may bear left here to follow the road back to the granite staircase and, eventually, your starting point.

Alternatively you may explore a little further by ascending the path from here, to the left of the stream, directly uphill. When it bifurcates bear right to follow a recently created path, with lots of newly planted trees, which follows a contour around a cleft in the valley side. This path will soon lead you back to the water spout at the roadside. Turn left and follow the road (or the hillside path you have just traversed) until you reach the granite staircase once more.

Climb the staircase to reach **Highview Lane**. Turn right at the end into **La Pouquelaye**, then right to **Grande Route de St Jean** and **B&Q**.

3 GRANDS VAUX
via Five Oaks, Grainville Playing Fields

This shortish walk explores a western corner of the parish of St Saviour. Grands Vaux is a major valley, part of which houses an eponymous reservoir fed by a stream flowing from Trinity to the north. The western side of the valley here is in the parish of St Helier – a typical example of a parish boundary being defined by a stream.

Distance:	3-4 kilometres	👢👢
Getting there:	Bus route No. 21	
Parking:	No parking; the nearby car park at Grainville Playing Fields is for patrons only; you risk having your vehicle wheel-clamped - you have been warned!	
Refreshment:	Five Oaks Hotel	

- From Five Oaks crossroads take the main road to St Helier, **Chemin de la Croix de Bois**, designated A7.

You walk past the attractively landscaped and solidly built Victoria Cottage Homes. These were opened in 1905 to mark Queen Victoria's Diamond Jubilee though only the three central blocks are of that vintage.

- Carry on past the turning to **Deloraine Road** and **Grainville Playing Fields** until you see **St Saviour's Parish Church** ahead. If you like poking around graveyards then this extensive example contains lots of interest, not least the grave of Lillie Langtry. This can be reached by passing through the gate ahead and walking straight on by the path. At the end turn left - you will find Lillie's grave on the right.

- On reaching the church turn right into **Rectory Lane**. You pass the original rectory on the left, where Lillie's father, William Corbet Le Breton, was formerly the incumbent. The lane soon reaches a crossroads - cross over and continue along **Swan Farm Lane**.

- At Swan Farm - now apparently residential - bear left by the way indicated as Public Footpath: Grands Vaux. The way bears right across fields before descending to the road beside **Grands Vaux Youth Centre** on the left and **Pillar Gardens** ahead.

- Stop here to ascertain the start of the next stage of the walk. You will find access to a footpath as it leaves the road by turning sharp right

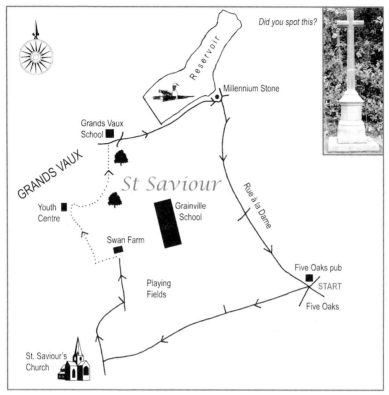

Did you spot this?

Millennium Stone

Reservoir

Grands Vaux
School

GRANDS VAUX

St Saviour

Youth
Centre

Grainville
School

Rue à la Dame

Swan Farm

Playing
Fields

Five Oaks pub

START

Five Oaks

St. Saviour's
Church

opposite the fenced, concreted play area below the Youth Centre. This path meanders between the boundary walls of the extensive estate of recently built dwellings to your left and the wooded slope to your right. You eventually meet the road opposite a pedestrian entrance to **Grands Vaux School.**

Turn right here, passing the foot of **Deloraine Road** and the dam which contains Grands Vaux Reservoir. At the next small junction marked by the foot of **Rue à la Dame**, there is a grassy triangle with a bench atop a mound which affords a view across the reservoir. This little oasis also provides a site for the **St Saviour Millennium Stone**.

You may care to rest here before tackling the final leg of the route which consists of the steady climb up **Rue à la Dame** to reach the crossroads at Five Oaks. Note the five oak trees which border the pub's car park.

17

4 LA HOUGUE BIE 1
via St Saviour's Hospital & Beuvelande Campsite

This is pleasant walk, largely in the eastern parishes of St Saviour and Grouville via quiet, undulating lanes and tracks. The first few hundred yards are along the fairly busy Route de la Hougue Bie. Refreshment in this inland part of the island is limited to the entrance hut at La Hougue Bie where you will at least be able to buy a coffee, but only between April and October when this site is open. A visit here is very well worthwhile as there is much of interest.

Distance:	5.5 kilometres	
Getting there:	Bus route No. 3A	
Parking:	Limited space on road outside, or inside if visiting	
Refreshment:	Limited to a drink at the entrance to La Hougue Bie in season – see above.	

- With your back to the entrance of La Hougue Bie turn right and carry straight on in an easterly direction along **Route de la Hougue Bie.** Do beware when negotiating the wide crossroads here – it's advisable to stick to the right-hand side of the road along this relatively busy route and, if there is more than one of you, to walk in single file.

- At the first crossroads marked by the entrance gate to the property known as **Tower Hamlet**, turn left into **Rue de la Hambie.** The way takes a right turn to pass **Aigretmont Farm**, then curves to the right. Head straight on along the indicated Public Footpath known as Hamlet Lane. Turn right at the end of the path then, at the T-junction, turn left along **Ruette des Ecorvées.** This is a green track between fields.

- Simply head straight on – you will see the spire of St Martin's Church across fields to your left. The farm track eventually becomes a metalled path defining the boundary between a large new residential development on the right facing open fields to the left. Turn right at the end of the new houses – the architecture here acknowledges the Jersey vernacular in the shape of a pair of semi-circular entrance arches heralding La Belle Vallette and Le Clos du Pressoir, both dated 2007. Join the main road opposite St Saviour's Hospital, whose imposing façade you will see across the road.

- Turn left – there is no pavement so take care as you make your way downhill. Take the first turning on your left: **Rue de la Chouquetterie.**

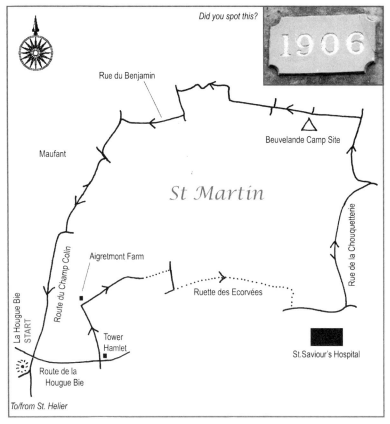

Did you spot this?

Rue du Benjamin

Maufant

St Martin

Beuvelande Camp Site

Rue de la Chouquetterie

Route du Champ Colin

Aigretmont Farm

Ruette des Ecorvées

La Hougue Bie
START

Tower
Hamlet

St.Saviour's Hospital

Route de la
Hougue Bie

To/from St. Helier

- The stream in the shallow valley to your right feeds into Queen's Valley
- Reservoir. The lane curves to the right at **Les Vaux Farm** and eventually
- meets a T-junction where you turn left via **Rue du Bouillon**. Next turn left
- into **Rue de Beuvelande** and head past Beuvelande Campsite. Continue
- past **Beauchamp Farm** and **Les Fontaines Farm** – note the fine old apple
- crusher in the garden.

- Carry on and turn left at the T-junction and soon take the first right. Exit
- **Rue du Benjamin** and turn left. The burgeoning built-up area known
- as Maufant is straight ahead. Turn left at **Rue de la Bachauderie** then
- immediately right into **Rue du Champ Colin**.

- Now simply follow this lane, turn right at the T-junction and immediately
- the lane curves left and eventually reaches the crossroads where you turn
- right and cross over for **La Hougue Bie**.

5 LA HOUGUE BIE 2
via Le Bourg and Le Boulivot

This is a very pleasant walk, largely in the south-eastern parish of Grouville via quiet lanes and a few short stretches off-road. There is one steep though brief climb. The first few hundred yards are via a B-road, the fairly busy Route de la Hougue Bie. There is a dearth of opportunities for refreshment in this inland part of the island being limited to the entrance hut at La Hougue Bie in season. A visit here, however, is well worthwhile as there is much of interest.

Distance:	5 kilometres
Getting there:	Bus route No. 3A
Parking:	Limited space on road outside, or inside if visiting
Refreshment:	Limited to a drink at the entrance to La Hougue Bie in season - see above.

- With your back to the entrance of La Hougue Bie turn right and carry straight on in as easterly direction along **Route de la Hougue Bie**. Do beware when negotiating the wide crossroads here - it's advisable to stick to the right-hand side of the road along this relatively busy route and, if there is more than one of you, to walk in single file.

- At the first crossroads turn right via **Le Catillon**. Take the first turning on the right - **La Hougue**. After about 100 metres, at a point where the lane curves to the right, look out for the beginning of a grassy track on the left.

This is a delightful stretch in the form of an unmade boundary path between fields. To the right is a shallow valley which marks the head of the valley which reaches down to Grouville Bay via Les Maltières.

- All too soon this grassy track ends at a metalled lane. Continue along here. At a point where the lane turns to the left you will no doubt wish to pause to take in the grand view which opens out.

- Carry on to drop down onto the main road, **Rue De Grouville**, and turn right. Very soon turn right into **Ruette Mathurin** and note the fine old lavoir on the right. The way now curves to the right and is overhung with trees and follows the valley to your right. Bear left and then turn right at the No Through Road sign.

- Follow this narrow way steeply uphill to the group of dwellings known

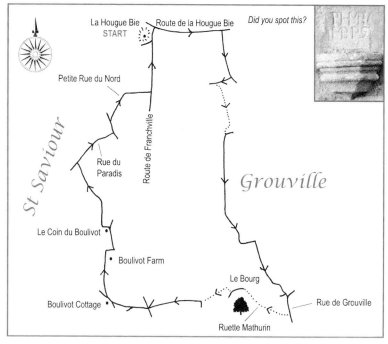

La Hougue Bie Route de la Hougue Bie *Did you spot this?*
START

Petite Rue du Nord

St Saviour

Route de Franchville

Rue du Paradis

Grouville

Le Coin du Boulivot

Boulivot Farm

Le Bourg

Boulivot Cottage

Rue de Grouville

Ruette Mathurin

• as Le Bourg. Bear right at the T-junction at **Le Bourg Cottages.**

• At the 5-way junction ahead you go straight across via **Le Boulivot de**
• **Bas.** The lane curves to the right at **Boulivot Cottage**. Now take the first
• on the right.

Across the fields to the left you look across St Clement's Bay – this high
spot in fact forms the watershed between streams flowing eastwards into
Grouville Bay, as we have seen, and those flowing south-west towards
St Clement's Bay.

• Boulivot Farm is on your right; once past you bear right, then very soon
• left and then left again at **Coin du Boulivot**. This narrow lane reaches
• a T-junction where you turn right. On meeting a further T-junction turn
• left. Soon you will see the entrance to a lane on the right. This is known
• as **Petite Rue du Nord**, whose naming presumably derives from the fact
• that this lane is tucked into a northern corner of the parish of Grouville,
• or that it heads out of the parish in a northerly direction.

• The lane ends at a junction where it joins **Route de Franchville**. Turn left
• here to reach the crossroads at **La Hougue Bi**e and the starting point.

6 GROUVILLE 1
via Fauvic and Coast Path

An easy walk on the level which takes in back lanes of Grouville and a section of the coast path beside Grouville Bay and passes much of interest en route.

Distance:	4 kilometres
Getting there:	Bus route No. 1, 1B & 2C
Parking:	There is some unrestricted parking space beside the war memorial opposite the Grouville Bus Shelter. An alternative would be the space, which appears to be not much used, beside the drive to the Golf Club by the apartments known as Chateau Royale.
Refreshment:	Pembroke pub
Note:	The final stage of the walk along the sea wall above Grouville Bay may be impassable at high tide so do check the likely state of the tide before you set out.

- Begin the walk by turning your back to the sculpture of Harry Vardon at the entrance drive to the **Royal Jersey Golf Club**. Cross the road into **Rue des Pres**. Take the road immediately to the left before the **Beausite Hotel**. Notice the house on the left known as La Gare, a former station on the Jersey Eastern Railway. Bear right at the end here and then left into a road indicated NO ENTRY.

- Head past **Grouville School** on your right and carry on until you reach the T-junction opposite **Clos de l'Eglise**. Turn left. Keep going, past the turning to the left. Exit **Rue des Fonds** and bear left into **Rue du Parcq**. At the junction ahead turn left into **Rue du Marais à la Cocque**.

You will not fail to notice the splendidly restored collection of artifacts on display here. The stepped pump, in particular, which its memorial tablet states was erected thus in 1930 by the tenants of Marais de la Cocque. Note also the spacious lavoir to the right which was refurbished as a millennium project for the parish.

- Head along the lane and look out for a pair of green and white banded posts on the right-hand side. These herald the course of a short stretch of footpath which holds a special interest. Turn right and head along this attractive, tree-lined way.

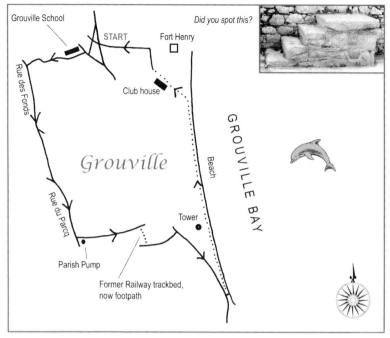

You will notice that the path is embanked and forms a kind of causeway above the low-lying fields on either side, remarkably like a railway embankment, you may surmise. And you would be right – the house opposite the end of this way, Old Station House, underlines the point!

- Turn left and exit **Rue de Fauvic** at the house called **Transvaal**. Turn right along the coast road with its intermittent pavement on the right. When the houses end on the coastward side, look out for a gap in the sea wall which gives access to steps down to a concrete apron at the foot of the sea wall (which may be covered at high tide - do beware!) and above the beach.

- Turn left and head along here until you reach a staircase just past the Martello Tower. Climb up here and follow the higher concrete path between the sloping sea wall and the houses. The concrete ends where the golf course begins. Bear left by the path toward the **Royal Jersey Golf Club** buildings and curve to the right of the apartments blocks to reach the main road and your starting point.

7 GROUVILLE 2
via Gorey Common, Royal Jersey Golf Club and Grouville Bay Coast Path

If you have an irrational fear of flying golf balls, this walk may not be for you, though the possibility of colliding with one is pretty slight. This is an easy walk on the level which, in part, follows the perimeter path of the golf course which the Royal Jersey Golf Club permits the public to use, so long as they do not stray from it onto the greens.

Distance:	4 kilometres	
Getting there:	Bus route No. 1, 1B & 2C	
Parking:	Large public car park beside road	
Refreshment:	Pembroke pub en route half way.	

- Begin on the pavement beside the bus stop on the Gorey village side of the car park. Head towards Gorey village by the road opposite the car park. Just before reaching the houses turn left along a path beside the stream on your right.

- Cross two minor roads and continue by the beaten path on the far side. At the fork bear right heading for the tall poplar trees ahead. Simply follow the beaten path as it bears left reach the road opposite an electricity sub-station. As you approach the edge of the open green, a notice forbids entry to the path through the trees, so bear left here to reach the pavement, then right for a short distance.

- Head just to the left of the sub-station by the beaten path and follow its course between the boundary fences of the properties on your right and the golf course to your left.

- Soon the path curves to the right, still following the boundary.

- The path now heads below some apartment blocks which overlook the golf course. A few yards to your left you pass a stone which commemorates **Harry Vardon, 1870-1937**, the famous Jersey golfer who, it informs, was born 'within putting distance' of this spot.

- Keep bearing right and, as you approach Green No. 15 on your right, leave the main path and fork to the right. As you emerge you head directly towards the statue of **Harry Vardon** at the entrance to the **Royal Jersey Golf Club**.

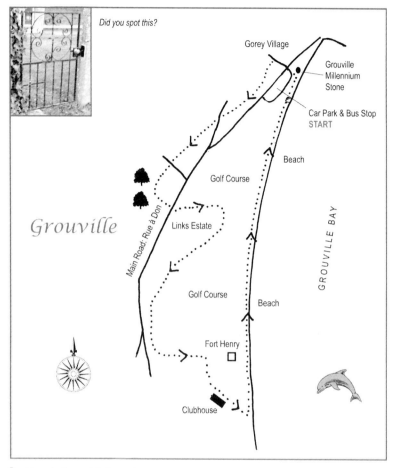

Did you spot this?

Gorey Village

Grouville Millennium Stone

Car Park & Bus Stop
START

Beach

Golf Course

Grouville

Main Road: Rue à Don

Links Estate

GROUVILLE BAY

Golf Course

Beach

Fort Henry

Clubhouse

Turn left and follow the drive to the Club buildings, then follow the grit path towards the beach. When you reach the sea wall turn left. Now follow the coast path beside the sea wall past a couple of Second World War gun emplacement and **Fort Henry** – notice the information board, just past the first German fortification, telling the story of Fort Henry.

Carry on beyond the golf course boundary until you reach the **Grouville Millennium Stone**. Bear left here and you will drop down to the car park and the main road where the buses stop on their way back to St Helier.

8 GOREY 1

via Mont de la Garenne, Gouray Church and Gorey Village

The initial steep climb rewards you with a panoramic view of Mont Orgueil Castle, Gorey Harbour and the sweep of Grouville Bay, before descending through the heart of Gorey village and heading back along the coast path.

Distance:	2 kilometres	👢👢
Getting there:	Bus route No. 1 & 1B	
Parking:	Limited parking at Gorey, much of which is restricted. The alternative is to use the car park beside the road opposite Gorey village.	
Refreshment:	Wide choice of cafés and restaurants at or close to Gorey Harbour.	

- To begin the walk: With your back to the terrace of buildings facing **Gorey Harbour** turn right, away from the harbour. Immediately past the public conveniences turn right and climb the path signposted in Jersey-French **P'tite Ruelle Muchie** leading to **Mont Orgueil Castle**.

- As you reach the top of the path bear left through the walled green, then up some steps on the right to reach the road below the **Castle Green** gastropub. Cross over and bear right up **Mont de la Garenne**, a steady climb. At the top bear left by a lane at the head of the steeply sloping field facing Mont Orgueil Castle.

This elevated way offers spectacular views towards the Castle and Gorey Harbour and across Grouville Bay to low-lying La Rocque, the south-west corner of Jersey, and Seymour Tower on a rock far offshore.

- This lane gives access to a few properties and then reverts to a footpath between boundary fences, then to a flight of steps, 56 in all, which drops you on to the road.

- Turn right here towards the spire of **Gouray Church**. At first there is a pavement on the right but this runs out where the road forks. Take the right fork - at this point it is perhaps advisable to cross over and walk along the left-hand side of the right-curving bend ahead.

- You draw near the entrance to the Church on the right. Opposite is a signposted 'Public Footpath to Gorey Village'. Descend the 38 steps and

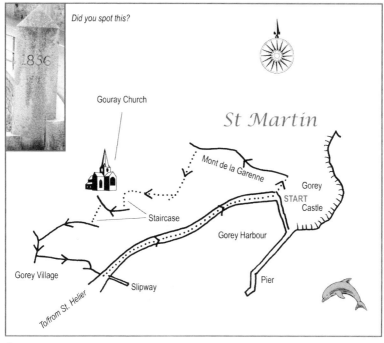

Did you spot this?

1856

Gouray Church

St Martin

Mont de la Garenne

Gorey
START
Castle

Staircase

Gorey Harbour

Gorey Village

Toll from St. Helier

Slipway

Pier

long slope until you reach the road below. Turn right past the entrance to **Gouray Lodge** signposted as 'Private' (in case you had any doubts).

Now bear left into the village – look out for the **Old Bank House** on your left. Take the first left along New Street with a row of single-storey former fishermen's cottages on the right.

These are a reminder of the nineteenth century heyday of the oyster fishing industry in Gorey which employed hundreds of local people.

Keep your eyes peeled for a narrow passage beside the house on the right named Homestead. Make your way along here to emerge at the end of Gorey Common. Turn left to follow the coast road and cross over to reach the slipway to the beach.

Now return to the harbour by the path between the sea wall and the gardens, along the course of the former railway line which ran from St Helier to Gorey Harbour.

9 GOREY 2
via Victoria Tower & Mont Mallet

This is a short route offering some off-road walking but, unavoidably, includes a short stretch via the pavementless coast road. As compensation, it takes in some spectacular views.

Distance:	1.5 kilometres
Getting there:	Bus routes No. 1 & 1B
Parking:	Limited parking at Gorey, much of which is restricted. The alternative is to use the car park beside the road opposite Gorey village.
Refreshment:	Wide choice of cafés and restaurants at or close to Gorey Harbour.

- To begin the walk: With your back to the terrace of buildings facing **Gorey Harbour** turn right, away from the harbour. Immediately past the public conveniences turn right and climb the path signposted in Jersey-French **P'tite Ruelle Muchie** rising to a track to **Mont Orgueil Castle**. Cross the track and continue by the steps opposite.

As you surmount the green below the castle you can take in the view north along the coast to St Catherine's Breakwater and east to the Normandy coast (if it's sufficiently clear).

- Make your way across the green and walk on beside the pavementless road, past the property known as **Roche du Lion**. You soon reach the headland signposted by the Jersey National Trust as Le Saut Geffroy - Jeffrey's Leap - with its view over the unspoilt bay of Anne Port.

- Just round the corner, beside the **road sign**, look out for a **JNT signpost** indicating the entrance to **Le Don Pilkington**. Follow this path as it twists and climbs its way uphill until you emerge from the trees. Carry on across the grass, to the left of **Victoria Tower**, to reach a track and an information board concerning the Tower. Bear right.

Now the view opens out on your left over the magnificent reach of Grouville Bay towards La Rocque at Jersey's south-east corner, with Seymour Tower perched on a rock a mile or so offshore.

- Head past **Old Cadet House**, with model canons perched on its gateposts, then **Seymour Farm** to reach a T-junction. If you turn right and walk along

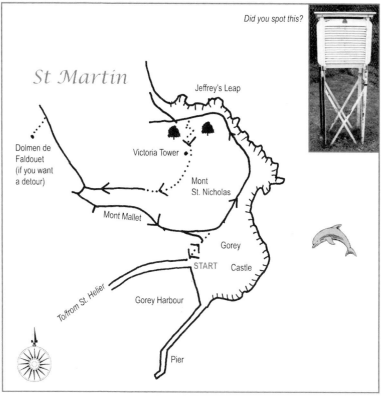

St Martin

Did you spot this?

Jeffrey's Leap

Dolmen de Faldouet (if you want a detour)

Victoria Tower

Mont St. Nicholas

Mont Mallet

Gorey

START   Castle

To/from St. Helier

Gorey Harbour

Pier

the lane for a few minutes you will reach the entrance path to **Dolmen de Faldouet** - a recommended detour.

Back at the junction, and with your back to the way you have come from Victoria Tower, turn left past **Pilot House** and then bear left to head downhill towards Mont Orgueil Castle. Take the NO ENTRY lane to the right of the entrance to the property named **Mont Mallet**.

This lane beside the côtil affords a wonderful vantage point (a bench is provided part way down) to take in the Castle, the Harbour, Grouville Bay and a wide expanse of sea (which in my view is at its best when the tide is up).

You emerge from this lane beside **Castle Green** gastropub on your left. Cross the road towards the steps opposite. Bear left here to reach the top of **P'tite Ruelle Muchie** and retrace your steps back down to **Gorey Harbour**, your starting point.

W A L K 9

10 ARCHIRONDEL

via Youth Hostel & Dolmen de Faldouet

A longish route along mainly quiet lanes exploring a corner of the predominantly rural parish of St Martin.

Distance:	5 kilometres
Getting there:	Bus route No. 1B
Parking:	Limited car parking beside the Café and beach
Refreshment:	Driftwood Café; Ransom's Garden Centre en route

Beside the **Driftwood Café**, with your back to the sea, climb up the road to reach the main road. Turn right and very soon left into **Rue des Landes**, indicated thus by a commemorative stone plaque set into the wall at the opposite corner. Begin climbing and look out for a narrow lane which loops off to the right and continue to climb. Exit **Vielle Charrière** and turn right.

At the staggered crossroads ahead turn left into **Rue de Basacre**. Turn right at the T-junction and then first left into **Rue des Alleurs** opposite the imposing house called **Springside**. Carry on past the turning for Rue du Bouillon and Rue du Ministre on the right. Exit **Chasse Mallet** by turning right and then sharp left. If you wish to stop at Ransom's Garden Centre then turn left here. Follow the road and you will find Ransom's on the left.

At the crossroads ahead, cross over the B28 and head along the lane signposted to Dolmen and Anne Port and indicated as **Rue de la Pouclée et des Quatre Chemins.**

Further along here the view opens out to the right, across Grouville Bay towards La Rocque, the low-lying south-west corner of the island. Nearer to hand, the spire of Gouray Church can be seen peeking above the far end of the fields.

You pass a rather impressive building to the right – this is Jersey's infamous Haut de la Garenne Children's Home whose image was beamed across the world when multiple cases of child abuse and even allegations of murder emerged in February 2008. You can see a memorial with a long list of names of former residents who died in the Great War. It provides a poignant reminder of an act of charity which rescued orphaned boys only for them to be sacrificed in the Great War.

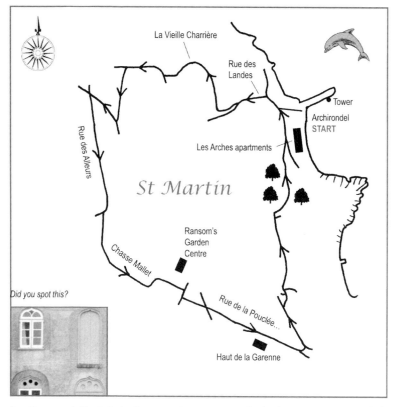

La Vieille Charrière

Rue des Landes

Tower

Archirondel
START

Les Arches apartments

Rue des Ailleurs

St Martín

Ransom's
Garden
Centre

Chasse Mallet

Did you spot this?

Rue de la Pouclée...

Haut de la Garenne

- Once past Haut de la Garenne (now unnamed) the lane swings to the left
- and your view switches northwards to St Catherine's Breakwater. You reach
- a minor junction with the entrance to a lane on the right.

A signpost here indicates access to Faldouet Dolmen a further 15 yards ahead – it's worth a short detour to view this impressive monument in its peaceful setting in a neatly hedged enclosure.

- Back at the minor junction turn down the lane towards Anne Port. Where
- it swings to the right carry straight on. You reach a junction of ways –
- Mont à la Crête is on the right. Don't turn down this lane but take the
- next turning on the right, at the head of a wooded valley, indicated **NO**
- **ENTRY**. This one-way lane provides a steep descent above the recently
- redeveloped Les Arches (now residential rather than an hotel) to the coast
- road below. Bear left and follow the road until you reach the lane down
- to Archirondel and the Driftwood Café.

11 St CATHERINE'S
via St Catherine's Valley

This walk is fairly demanding, including as it does several steady ascents. It is, nevertheless, a fine route with much off-road walking.

Distance:	4.5 kilometres	
Getting there:	Bus route No. 1B	
Parking:	There is adequate parking space at the head of the breakwater or on the approach road.	
Refreshment:	Breakwater Café	

- To begin the walk: Facing the sea and with your back to the **Breakwater Café** at St Catherine's, turn right. Walk past **Jersey Turbot**, a reinvention of a former World War 2 bunker. Where the road bifurcates, at the end of the boat park, look out for the start of the coast path to your left. Drop down steps and follow the path along the top of the sea wall and beside the road.

- When you emerge above a slipway down to the beach, look out for a roadsign indicating **B91 to Rozel**. Now walk along the roadside. Cross over and head up this one-way lane, past the large house on the right known as **Bel Val**.

- Bear left on reaching the T-junction at the summit and begin to descend – there is a good view from here down to the Martello Tower at La Mare and across to another at Archirondel.

- In the dip you are at the mouth of St. Catherine's Valley. Turn right at the crossroads along the **B62 to St Martin's Church**. After a short distance turn right into the lane signposted as **Rue des Charrières**.

- Follow the lane through a hairpin bend ignoring the tempting path which heads down into the woods at this point. Carry on climbing until the way levels out. Pass a couple of houses and a turning on the left. Look out for the beginning of a path on the right; it is clearly signposted **Ruette de Quatre Pieds: Footpath to St Catherine**. (When I rewalked this route in January 2010, the signpost had vanished. The entrance to the footpath will be found just before a lane turning to the right).

- Follow this fenced path between fields – you may see sheep in the

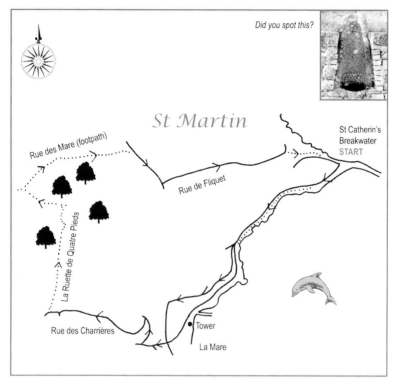

Did you spot this?

St Martin

Rue des Mare (footpath)

Rue de Fliquet

La Ruette de Quatre Pieds

Rue des Charrières

Tower

La Mare

St Catherin's
Breakwater
START

fields to the left; also the battlemented Rozel Manor and the spire of St Martin's Church. As the path enters the woods it begins to descend. The way is fairly clear but, if in doubt, keep bearing to the left.

At the valley floor turn left and follow the footpath.

At a Y-junction of paths bear right. Then, at the T-junction of paths a little further on, turn right across the stream and up the deep, walled way. As you climb out of the trees there is a view across the fields on the left towards **Rozel Manor**. Now follow the level path between fields until you reach the track which serves a number of dwellings close to the main road. Turn right at the road.

Take the next turning on the left which is signposted **Rue de Flicquet** - note the Victorian letterbox set into the garden wall opposite. When the lane curves to the left carry straight on by the path signposted **Ruette du Verclut: Footpath to St Catherine**. Join the road below and carry on to the **Breakwater Café**.

12 ROZEL

via La Vallée de Rozel & the Dolmen du Couperon

The well-wooded north-east corner of the island is explored in the course this walk. There is a steady climb from Rozel and another from the dolmen – hence the 3-boot category – but the route provides much variety and combines sea and countryside.

Distance:	4 kilometres	
Getting there:	Bus route No. 3	
Parking:	Parking is very limited at Rozel; best to use the bus.	
Refreshment:	The Rozel pub and the Hungry Man Café on the pier.	

- To begin the walk locate the crossroads at **Brecque du Sud** (opening to the beach) - at the foot of the hill coming from St Helier. With your back to the sea at La Brecque du Sud head along the road opposite, past **The Rozel** bar and restaurant, the **Bus Terminus** on the left and **Chateau La Chaire Hotel** on the right.

Note that the walls here are not built of granite but of rough-hewn blocks of the local Rozel Conglomerate rock.

- The lane bears left at the entrance to Les Vaux. This lane - **Vallée de Rozel** - climbs steadily, eventually reaching the house called **Haut de la Vallée** where, thankfully, the way begins to levels out. At the T-junction turn left. The level lane gives big seaward views, then gradually descends to meet the road. Exit **Rue de Caen** and turn right.

- You soon turn left along the road signposted to Fliquet and St. Catherine's. Across the field to the right you will see the turreted pile of **Rozel Manor**. At the next junction turn left into **Rue du Scez**. which takes a right turn, then a left. Head straight on at the next minor junction following signpost to La Saie Harbour. This lane soon descends into a wooded valley, a delightful place under the care of the Jersey National Trust.

You will see their attractive signpost on the right. This land is known as Le Grand Côtil de la Côte Pallot and was purchased in 1938 through public subscription so is one of its first acquisitions, the Trust having been founded two years previously. The headland – La Coupe, surmounted by its white navigation mark away to the right – was gifted to the Trust in

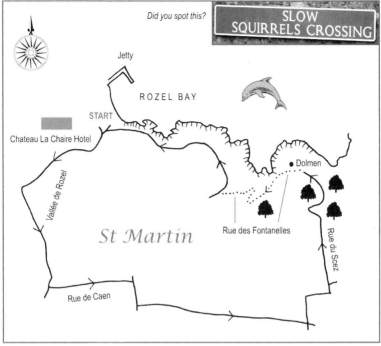

2004. It's a shame that there is no footpath through the wooded slopes to link the two sites.

- Continue by the lane until you reach a track on the left signposted as **Rue des Fontenelles** and then a small car park. At the far side of the car park bear left to follow the field edge to reach an information board describing the dolmen at the head of the field. The old hut also bears an information board describing at as **Le Couperon Guardhouse**. Beside the hut is **Dolmen du Couperon**, an ancient and rather mutilated burial chamber. Before heading off on the next stage of the walk it is worth climbing up to the little headland behind the hut to take in the view – towards La Coupe Point to the east and Rozel Harbour to the west.

- From the Dolmen head towards **Rue des Fontenelles**. Follow the track uphill to reach the main road.

- At the road – **Le Mont de Rozel** – turn right. The way, once past the large new dwelling named **Harleyford**, is deeply incised in the Rozel Conglomerate before making its steady descent to the Bay and your starting point.

13 St MARTIN
via Green Lanes & head of St Catherine's Valley

This is a pleasant walk along quiet country lanes in the parish of St Martin, much of it around the head of the valley which drains into St. Catherine's Bay to the east.

Distance:	4.5 kilometres
Getting there:	Bus route No. 3, 3A, 23
Parking:	Large car park opposite the Parish Hall
Refreshment:	The Royal pub; Village Tea Room

- Facing the **Parish Hall** bear right and turn left into **Rue des Raisies**. Looking across the fields to the right you will see, on a clear day, the coast of France on the horizon. The lane twists and turns and dips into a shallow valley - this is near the head of St Catherine's Valley - until reaching a T-junction where you exit **Rue du Puchot** and turn right.

- At the junction ahead bear left at **Westlea**, then the road curves first to the right, then to the left. At this point turn right into **Rue de la Ville Brée** and continue along the lane.

Note the thatched house on the left – once commonplace in country districts of the island but now a rare sight.

- The lane bears right at **Holmdale** - note the dwelling's marriage stone dated 1822. La Rue de la Ville Brée now becomes **La Rue du Rât** and offers wide-ranging views towards France and the Ecréhous which belong to the Parish of St Martin. The lane takes a right turn, then a left, then again a right.

Note the stone tower across the field to the left – this is the stump of the former Rozel windmill – with signs that the Germans included it in their island fortifications.

- At the T-junction turn left along **Rue des Alleurs**. This is a designated B-road but is relatively quiet. Across the fields to your right you will spot the spire of St Martin's Church. You pass **Rue du Moulin** to the left. Just beyond Forge Cottage you take a right turn into **Rue du Blanc Pignon**. This becomes **Rue de la Palloterie** as it dips once again into the beginnings of St Catherine's Valley.

- You reach a T-junction to meet **Grande Route de Rozel**. To the left is a

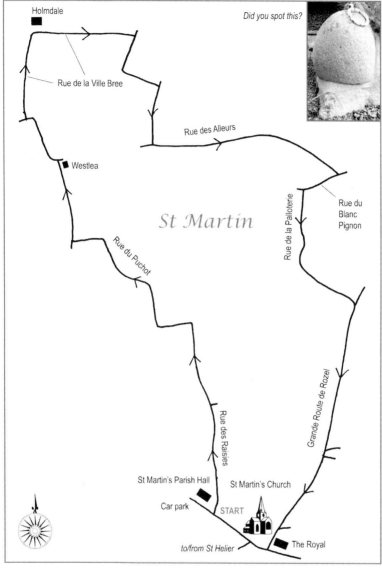

Holmdale

Did you spot this?

Rue de la Ville Bree

Rue des Alleurs

Westlea

St Martin

Rue de la Pallotere

Rue du Blanc Pignon

Rue du Puchot

Grande Route de Rozel

Rue des Raisies

St Martin's Parish Hall

St Martin's Church

Car park

START

to/from St Helier

The Royal

- fenced bridge across the well-wooded valley. Turn right and follow the
- road into St. Martin. At the junction the church is on your right, the pub
- on the left. Further along to the right you will reach the **Parish Hall**.

14 TRINITY 1
via Bouley Bay Hill & Jardin d'Olivet

This walk is largely off-road and includes some footpaths around the wooded heights, known as Jardin d'Olivet, which lead to Trinity's rocky, north-facing coast. This is common land and the route will introduce you to this natural habitat. This short walk could be linked with Walk 14.

Distance:	2 - 3 kilometres
Getting there:	Bus route 4
Parking:	Parc de la Petite Falaise in Rue de la Petite Falaise
Refreshment:	Trinity Arms pub

- Start from the Trinity Arms (if arriving by bus): With your back to the **Trinity Arms**, turn left and then right at the AA box into **Rue du Presbytère**. You can avoid a stretch of road walking by entering the churchyard at the lych gate and bearing right, through the churchyard to find the road which will take you past the **Parish Hall**. Turn right at the T-junction at **Rue de la Petite Falaise**. Carry on past **Rue des Fontaine**s on your left until you reach the car park on your left at **Parc de la Petite Falaise**.

- Start from **Parc de la Petite Falaise** (if arriving by car):

- *Route 1:* This is a very brief walk but does offer spectacular views on the initial descent. From the car park bear right into the field and immediately left in a seaward direction towards the gap in the hedge below. Once through here follow the path beside the gorse on your right to reach a flight of 38 concrete steps. This is a great vantage point with views down and across Bouley Bay. At the road below cross straight over to reach a further flight of steps, 56 or thereabouts. Cross the road once more to reach a track through the woods.

- *Route 2:* This a rather longer route. After turning into **Rue de la Petite Falaise**, turn left into **Rue de la Fontaine**. Follow this winding lane until you reach a fork where you bear right. This lane merges into **Rue de l'Epine** - a quiet, tree-shrouded lane which descends the wooded hillside. At the foot bear right until you meet **Charrières de Bouley**, the road leading to and from Bouley Bay. Bear right once more - notice the lavoir, dated 1834, on the grassy bank to your right. At the hairpin bend ahead go straight ahead via a narrow track leading into the woods.

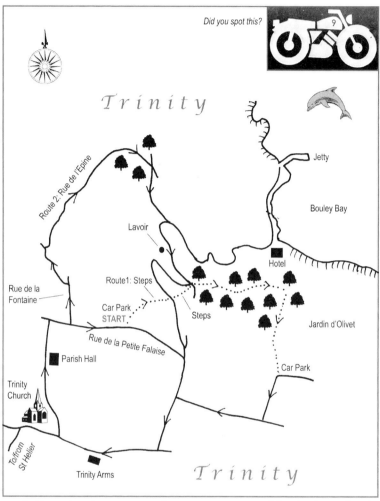

Did you spot this?

Trinity

Route 2: Rue de l'Epine

Jetty

Bouley Bay

Lavoir

Route1: Steps

Hotel

Rue de la Fontaine

Car Park
START

Steps

Jardin d'Olivet

Rue de la Petite Falaise

Parish Hall

Car Park

Trinity Church

To/from St Helier

Trinity Arms

Trinity

- **Both routes:** Ignore a set of gateposts on your right. Look out for the indicated Coastal Path to Bouley Bay and Rozel and carry on.

- When you reach a fork bear right (the left-hand path zigzags downhill to join the coast path to Bouley Bay) and follow the path through woods. It eventually swings to the right and begins to climb quite steeply (notice the recently restored folly on your right) until it delivers you at a car par. Carry on to reach the road; turn right at the T-junction with **Chemin d'Olivet**. Turn left at the next T-junction to reach the **Trinity Arms**; turn right and left via **Rue de la Petite Falaise** to reach the car park.

15 TRINITY 2
via Jardin d'Olivet & Coast Path

This short walk is largely off-road and includes a stretch of the North Coast Path and some footpaths around the gorse-clad heights, known as Jardin d'Olivet, which lead to Trinity's rocky, north-facing coast. This is common land and this route will take you to the best it has to offer.

Distance:	1.5 kilometres
Getting there:	Bus route 4
Parking:	Car park beside Chemin d'Olivet
Refreshment:	Trinity Arms pub

- Start from the Trinity Arms (if arriving by bus): With your back to the **Trinity Arms** pub turn right, then left into **Route du Boulay**, right along **Chemin d'Olivet** and first left. This will lead you to a car park.

- Start from car park **Chemin d'Olivet** (if arriving by car).

- Head across the car park to the far right corner and follow the beaten path which leads off from this point. Head towards the two bench seats which are ideally positioned to take in the sweeping view down to Bouley Bay and the headland beyond.

- Head back to the main path and bear left to follow a course parallel with the cliff edge. When you reach a fork bear left in a seaward direction. You soon descend through gorse and heather-clad slopes to reach a junction with the coast path; at this point indication is given of the distances to Bouley Bay and eastwards to Rozel.

- Bear right and drop down to reach a wooden footbridge. Cross over and continue up the coast path until you reach a bench seat, then a second bench seat, both of which provide fine viewpoints. Notice the granite sign beside the second bench which indicates a footpath to the right leading to the main road in 400 yards.

- Follow this path until you reach the top of a flight of steps. Carry on for a few minutes. At a junction of paths look out for an indicated **Bridleway** – turn right here and descend to cross a stream. Clamber up the far side and bear left via the beaten path beside the stream to your left.

- Keep going up here until you reach the drive to a house, then carry on

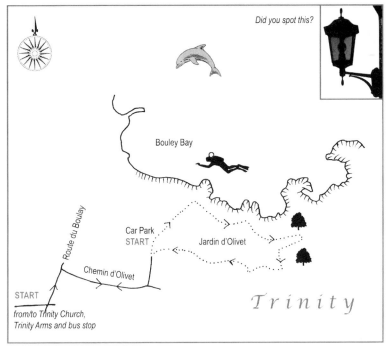

Did you spot this?

Bouley Bay

Route du Boulay

Car Park
START

Jardin d'Olivet

Chemin d'Olivet

START

from/to Trinity Church,
Trinity Arms and bus stop

Trinity

- across the open area with the fenced drive away to your left. You will reach a gorse-enclosed field and see the car park straight ahead.

- If you arrived by bus then you need to retrace your steps by turning right into **Chemin d'Olivet**, left into **Route du Boulay** and finally right at the main road.

A battle was fought at Jardin d'Olivet in 1549. I am grateful to Sidney Bisson's account in his book *Jersey Our Island* (Batchworth Press, 1950): 'The Jersey Militia, assisted (according to some accounts) by an English naval squadron, defeated a French expeditionary force which had landed at Bouley Bay in one of France's many attempts to annex the island. If the figures given by the old chroniclers are to be believed, it was a much bloodier encounter than the better known Battle of Jersey in 1781. A thousand Frenchmen are reputed to have fallen. When he heard the news, Henri II, King of France, forbad his courtiers ever to mention Jersey again in his presence.'

16 TRINITY 3
via Millennium Walk, Le Don Huelin & Mont Pellier

This is an enjoyable ramble around quiet lanes and along some recently created off-road footpaths.

Distance:	4 kilometres	
Getting there:	Bus route 4	
Parking:	Limited parking on main road near shop & pub; Parish Hall on the right of the road north of the church.	
Refreshment:	Trinity Arms pub	

- With your back to the **Trinity Arms** turn right and right again at **Les Maisons Cabot** along **Verte Rue**. Pass by **Rue du Travers** on the right and fork left along **Rue du Câtel**.

- On reaching the T-junction at **Le Câtel Farm** turn right. At the next T-junction bear right and then sharp left opposite **Les Câteaux** – note the neat set of mounting steps here. You are now walking along **Rue des Câteaux** though this is not indicated.

- The lane begins to descend to a wooded valley – this is the beginning of Grand Vaux; the stream in the valley bottom feeds the reservoir to the south. Look out for **Rue du Pouillier**, otherwise known as **Millennium Walk**, signposted on the right. You now forsake tarmac for a welcome stretch of off-road walking along what soon becomes a boundary path between fields. This way can be muddy after rain and the churning effect of horses' hooves. It levels out and then descends a little to reach **Verte Rue**. Now turn right to reach the minor junction below.

- To the left is **Rue du Moulin de Bas**; however, at this junction there is the entrance to a footpath through woods. Head for the stile opposite signposted **Ruelle ès Biches**. Follow the path down to a bridge across a stream which is dammed to the left. Proceed up the far side – note the farmhouse to your right with its fine belfry.

- Follow the path ahead to the field boundary where you bear right until the right of way strikes off to the left to descend by a sunken way. Note the waterwheel in the grounds of the property on the far side of the lane as you descend to emerge from **Ruelle ès Biches** at a crossroads.

- Turn right here along **Rue du Mont Pellier**. You pass some particularly

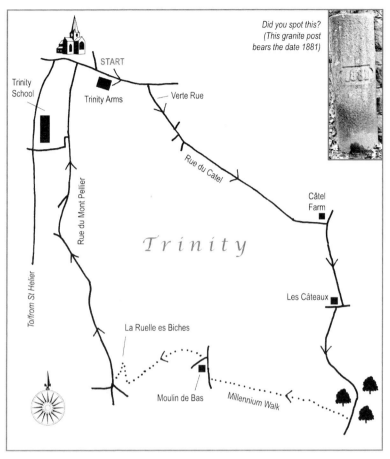

Did you spot this?
(This granite post
bears the date 1881)

START

Trinity
School

Trinity Arms

Verte Rue

Rue du Catel

Câtel
Farm

Trinity

Rue du Mont Pellier

To/from St Helier

Les Câteaux

La Ruelle es Biches

Moulin de Bas

Millennium Walk

- marshy ground on your left, then the entrance to **Mont Pellier** with its
- impressive entrance arch bearing the date 1686.

Trinity School can be seen across the valley to the left. On the right, beyond Rue du Travers, you pass a track which leads to a field and the 'Jersey Cider Apple Collection' – an orchard planted in 1991 with traditional Jersey cider Apple varieties following the Great Storm of 1987 which destroyed many of Jersey's remaining cider apple trees.

- You emerge on to the main road opposite **Trinity Church**; bear right to
- reach **Trinity Arms** pub, or right and sharp left for the Parish Hall.

17 UNION INN
via Sion & Island Centre Stone

This route ventures into lanes and footpaths either side of the road which heads due north from St Helier to St John and includes the stone which is reputed to mark the centre of the island.

Distance:	3 kilometres	
Getting there:	Bus route 5	
Parking:	No public parking so best to arrive by bus (or you ask in the Union Inn for permission to use their car park, but only if you intend making it a stop for refreshment)	
Refreshment:	Union Inn; Rondel's Farm Shop	

- With your back to the Union Inn, turn right. Cross the main road to take the first on the left: **Rue des Arbres**. Head along this lane – you will pass a tempting looking lane on the right leading down to Vallée des Vaux. However, our route continues as the lane bears to the left to join Rue du Becquet Vincent on the left.

- Head straight on along **Rue de la Garenne**. The lane soon bears right; at this point look out for a track to the left heralded by NO WAITING and Dead End signs. Go down here and make for the footpath which leads off just to the left of the house. Follow this boundary path between fields.

- At the lane continue in the same direction, to the left of **Maison de Bas** between dwellings, until you reach a further boundary path with a watercourse on the left.

- Emerge at a lane and turn left until you reach the junction with **Rue du Douet**. Continue in the same direction, past the turning to the right, intriguingly named **Rue du Poivre**, until you approach the main road with **Macpela Cemetery** on your right.

This cemetery comprises a small field beside the road. This built-up area is known as Sion Village, taking its name from the Sion Methodist Church beside the road at the community's southern end. The village has neither school nor pub but does have a shop and garage.

- Turn left at the main road. A short diversion can be made by crossing the road and heading along **Rue des Servais** to reach the Island Centre Stone.

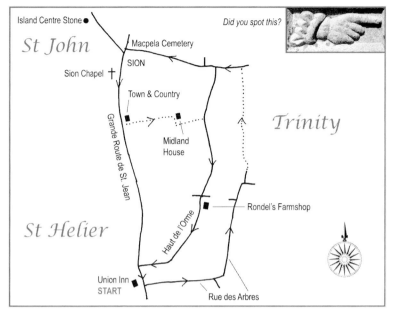

The Island Centre Stone is found after a hundred metres or so, past Centre House, beside the lane on the left at the entrance to Les Chasses.

- Return to the main road and turn right where a pavement on the far side will lead you past **Sion Methodist Church**. Carry on until you reach the Town and Country Filling Station and shop. Turn left along the drive immediately beyond, signposted to Midland House. As you approach the big house, the way turns right and then left and finally drops you onto Rue du Douet. Here turn right, past some fine houses, to reach a crossroads. Head across the staggered junction via **Rue de Haut de l'Orme**.

This higher ground affords a distant view to the right over much of the western half of the island. You pass an extensive range of old farm buildings here, including Rondel's Farm Shop.

- Now simply carry on, bearing right, until you reach the main road with the **Union Inn** opposite.

18 St LAWRENCE

via Green Lanes, Le Rât Cottage & Morel Farm

This a pleasant route which follows mainly quiet Green Lanes in the central parish of St Lawrence, the calm heart of Jersey with its distinctively rural character. There is a moderate descent and ascent in the middle of the route.

Distance:	5 kilometres	
Getting there:	Bus routes 7. 7a, 7b	
Parking:	Usually space to park in road round churchyard	
Refreshment:	British Union pub at start/finish point;	
	Jersey War Tunnels Café en route	

- To begin the walk: Head along the lane, in a northerly direction, behind **St Lawrence Church**; this is **Route de l'Eglise**. This quiet way runs parallel to the main road away to the right.

- You pass the turning for Mont Perrine on the left but take the next left to descend **Mont l'Evesque**.

As you reach the foot of the hill look out for a charming old cottage on the right. This is Le Rât Cottage, owned and cared for by the Jersey National Trust.

- At this building's end you pass Mont Perrine to the left. Bear right via **Rue de la Fontaine St Martin**, passing an abreuvoir at the lowest point and Mont Isaac to the right. Just before you reach the junction you pass Morel Farm.

Morel is a fine, traditional Jersey farm also looked after by the Jersey National Trust. You will note the belfry atop the barn beside the lane, then the arched entrances, the main one bearing the date 1666, to the farmhouse.

- Bear left at the T-junction via **Les Charrières Malorey**, then continue via **Chemin des Montagnes**.

Once again the saddle-back tower of St Lawrence Church is in view across the fields, plus the pointed tower of the Parish Hall to its left.

- Chemin des Montagnes curves right and again right to pass the modest dwelling known as **Les Grands Montagnes**.

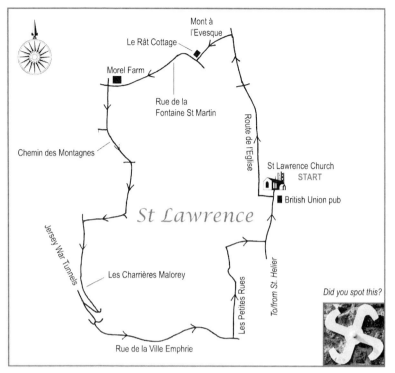

At the T-junction you leave **Chemin des Montagnes**, turn left and descend steadily. You reach a hairpin bend to the right to reach the end of Les **Charrières Malorey** at a T-junction. **Jersey War Tunnels** is a short distance up the road to your right.

However, to continue the walk, bear left by the pavement. The road soon curves to the right via Rue des Pres Sorsoleil but we carry straight on, climbing steadily, up **Rue de la Ville Emphrie**. You pass **La Ville Emphrie** with a stone well and pump opposite and then a second dwelling bearing the same name (?!)

As the road levels out at a minor crossroads you turn left along **Les Petites Rues**. After a dogleg bend you can look across the fields to the left to see the distant spire of St Peter's Church. This lane eventually bears right to reach the main road at the entrance to **Le Colombier Manor**. Turn left here – look out for a gap in the wall to enter a grassy field. Now follow the beaten path beside the wall until you reach the grit path through the graveyard to reach the lane beside the church.

19 HAMPTONNE
via Sentier des Moulins & Handois

A short, quiet route by path and lane in the attractive interior of St Lawrence. Hamptonne Country Life Museum is a delightful place to visit and very informative of Jersey's rural tradition.

Distance:	2.5 kilometres 👢 👢
Getting there:	Bus route No. 7, 7a, 7b. Alight at Three Oaks and from here head along Rue des Corvées, turn right into Chemin de Moulins and finally left into Rue de la Patente.
Parking:	There is usually ample space in the area reserved for car parking in the field above Hamptonne though you are advised to request permission to do so at the entrance desk.
Refreshment:	Hamptonne has a café. Sadly, since 2010, this wonderful museum is open only on special days during the summer months.

- To begin the walk: with your back to Hamptonne turn left downhill. At the T-junction turn left down **Chemin des Moulins**, past the square dovecote on your right.

- At the foot of the slope, at a point where the lane swings off to the right, look out for a Footpath sign beside the road to your left. Turn left via the path which a sign here indicates has been gifted to the Jersey National Trust. Follow this path up valley.

- You reach the road at Mont Gavey opposite a former mill – Le Moulin de Quétivel – which has been sited here for around 700 years.

- Continue the walk by heading along the lane opposite, **Rue Ville es Gazeaux**. Look back and to the left to see the old overshot waterwheel.

- A stream runs at the left side beside the lane. A footprint sign indicates that the route heads to the left to follow the stream more closely, then briefly crosses to the left side, then back to the right side to follow a fence. You leave this path as you reach an information board with details about the China Clay Quarries which were formerly situated hereabouts. You join a lane which curves to the left below the dam at Handois Reservoir.

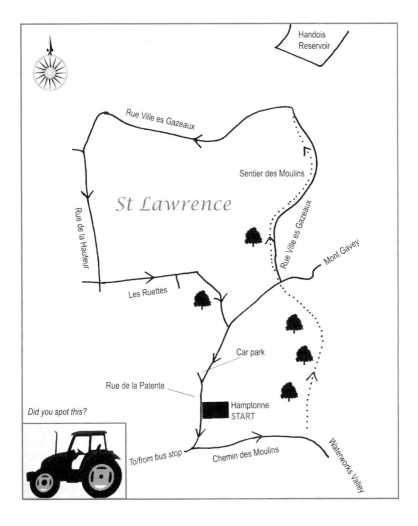

Handois
Reservoir

Rue Ville es Gazeaux

Sentier des Moulins

St Lawrence

Rue de la Hauteur

Rue Ville es Gazeaux

Mont Gavey

Les Ruettes

Car park

Rue de la Patente

Hamptonne
START

Did you spot this?

To/from bus stop

Chemin des Moulins

Waterworks Valley

- You pass China Quarries on your right to reach a minor junction with **Fraide Rue** to the right. Bear left along Rue de la Hauteur.

- At the crossroads turn left into Les Ruettes and then take the second right. At the T-junction turn right along the lane which will take you back to Hamptonne and your starting point.

20 St MARY 1
via Les Charrièrres Country Hotel & The Elms

A longish but varied walk along quiet lanes though there is one unavoidable stretch along a B-road.

Distance:	5 kilometres	👢👢
Getting there:	Bus routes 7, 7a, 7b	
Parking:	Parish Hall	
Refreshment:	Parish Hall and school	

- To begin the walk: With your back to the **Parish Hall** and **School**, cross the road and bear left via the footpath beside the road to reach the crossroads. Turn right into **Route de L'Eglise** to reach **St Mary's Country Inn**. Cross the road, go through the gate to the churchyard and bear right beside the church. Exit the churchyard to join **Route de Ste Marie**. Look out for the first turning on the left, **Rue és Viberts**, and proceed along this twisty way.

- At the end of **Rue és Viberts** turn left along the main road; proceeding in single file is advisable here – do take care. At the junction of five ways, turn left along the lane indicated **Rue des Sillons**.

- As you approach **Les Charrières Country Hotel** on the right look left towards the quarry and the spire of St John's Church in the distance. There follows a sharp descent down **Mont des Charrières**. At the foot bear left, past the lane known as La Dimerie. Note the watercourse here – a mill leat which once drove the wheel of nearby Gigoulande Mill, now a hidden ruin.

- Cross the road, with care, beside the offices of the granite quarry and climb the lane opposite, indicated **Mont Remon**. The chain link fence on your left follows the boundary of the quarry workings. As the lane levels out carry straight on via **Rue Bechervaise**. This lonely lane reaches a T-junction where you turn left.

- Continue along **Chêve Rue**. Once past Rue à Georges, the lane becomes deeply sunken as it descends to emerge into an open valley. To the right is the grand house **Beau Pré**; further along to the right is **The Elms**, the handsome headquarters of the National Trust for Jersey.

- Pass through the pair of low white gates immediately beyond the entrance to **Beau Prè**. Follow the track ahead until you reach a crossing of tracks;

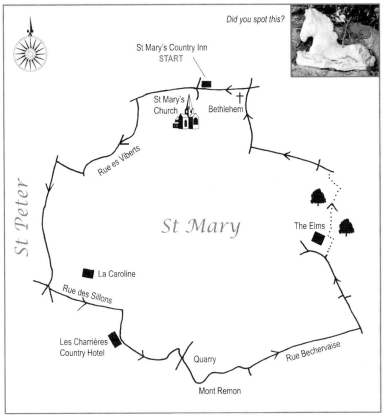

Did you spot this?

St Mary's Country Inn
START

St Mary's
Church

Bethlehem

Rue es Viberts

St Peter

St Mary

The Elms

La Caroline

Rue des Sillons

Les Charrières
Country Hotel

Quarry

Rue Bechervaise

Mont Remon

turn left here towards the arch in the boundary wall of The Elms. Turn right through the 5-bar gate and follow the beaten path to the left of the stream. At the second footprint post bear left up a flight of 34 steps. Go through the gate here and follow the field boundary to a second gate. Once through here look out for a footprint post a few metres further along. Bear right and descend the steps to a boundary path. Bear right towards an impressive round arch. Threatening notices will deter you from entering this private domain which was once Perry Farm.

Turn left along the lane known as La Rue du Maistre, or Perry Farm Lane, from where you will see the spire of St Mary's Church ahead, to reach **Rue de la Rosière**. Turn right and walk up to the junction where you turn left beside **Bethlehem Methodist Church**. Cross the road, with care, to use the pavement on the far side in order to reach your starting point at St Mary's Country Inn.

21 St MARY 2

via Green Lanes & La Hougue Mauger

This is a level walk along quiet lanes in the northerly St Mary's Parish. with views across the sea towards Sark and other Channel Islands.

Distance:	4 kilometres	
Getting there:	Bus routes 7, 7a, 7b	
Parking:	Parish Hall	
Refreshment:	Parish Hall and School	

- To begin the Walk: With your back to the **Parish Hall** and **School**, cross the road and bear left via the footpath beside the road to reach the crossroads.

Note the parish primary school, Ecole Elementaire, with its separate entrances for Filles (Girls) and Garçons (Boys). All these parish buildings are painted blue and white, the colours of St Mary's. The modern school sign is bilingual, not English and French but English and Jersey French: 'L'École dé Sainte Mathie'. When the school was built, in 1901, Jersey French was actively discouraged and a school sign in the language would not have been considered.

- Turn right at the crossroads into **Route de L'Eglise** to reach **St Mary's Country Inn**.

- Now with your back to **St Mary's Country Inn**, bear left and turn down the first turning on the left, **Rue de la Rosière**. At the junction, cross over to follow **Rue du Motier**. This way soon becomes sunken and overarched with trees growing from the banks on either side.

- At the minor junction ahead – La Rue des Marais is to the left – carry straight on by what appears to be someone's drive but soon leads to a bridleway. Once past the house, **Champs Verts**, the way becomes a track between fields, then reverts to a path between hedgerows.

- On reaching a lane, turn left until you reach a minor junction at the house named **La Hougue Mauger**.

A hougue is an ancient burial place of which there are many in Jersey. Here, however, there are no remains visible from the road.

- Continue along **Rue des Touettes**, a high and lonely lane.

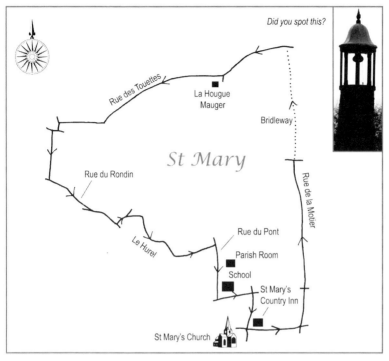

Did you spot this?

Rue des Touettes

La Hougue
Mauger

Bridleway

St Mary

Rue du Rondin

Rue de la Motier

Le Hurel

Rue du Pont

Parish Room

School

St Mary's
Country Inn

St Mary's Church

Take in the view to the right and northwards – across the sea to Sark on the horizon and the Paternoster rocks closer to hand.

- At the end of this lane bear right and sharp left. The lane soon bears left amongst a concentration of housing, some old, some more recent – to emerge above a cotîl (steeply sloping field) which looks across the top end of the well wooded Grève de Lecq Valley.

- Exit **Rue du Rondin**. After a further 50 metres or so, turn left into **La Charrière**, then very soon right into **Le Hurel** which you follow towards the village of St Mary. At the T-junction turn right into Rue du Pont.

The Pont, or bridge, is to the left at the foot of this lane and crosses a branch of the stream that flows into Grève de Lecq valley.

- You now approach, to your left, the recently built, blue-tinted glass St Mary's Community Centre. Behind the Community Centre you reach your starting point – the Salle Paroissiale, **Parish Hall** – dated 1879. Note the commemorative stones set around the flagpole, dedicated to mark the 50th and 60th anniversary of the Liberation.

53

22 GRÈVE DE LECQ 1
via Chemin du Câtel & Grève de Lecq Valley

A steep climb, a level walk with views over Grève de Lecq Valley, followed by a steep (and possibly prickly) descent; finally a shady woodland walk to return to the starting point.

Distance:	2.5 kilometres	
Getting there:	Bus routes 7b, 9	
Parking:	There is usually ample space either in the car park surrounding the Martello Tower or in the one above the Romany Café.	
Refreshment:	Pubs include the Prince of Wales and the Moulin de Lecq (just uphill on the right along Le Mont de Ste. Marie); cafès are the Romany and, further along the sea wall to the left, Colleen's.	
Note:	The footpath downhill from Chemin du Câtel may be hedged in with brambles and nettles in summer months so bare legs could mean a painful encounter.	

• To begin the walk, take the narrow lane, **Chemin du Câtel**, which you
• find behind the bus stop, telephone kiosk and St Mary's Millennium Cross
• and below Grève de Lecq Barracks.

Construction of Grève de Lecq Barracks was begun in 1810 against the threat from Napoleon and was designed to house 250 troops. It is now beautifully preserved under the auspices of the Jersey National Trust and houses an exhibition on Jersey's spectacular north coast when open in the summer months.

• This gradually climbs the hillside and swings to the right by the entrance
• track to **Le Câtel Fort**. This is worth a detour though the gates to the
• fortified enclosure are usually padlocked. However, there is a vantage
• point beside the fort which affords a great view across the bay.

As the lane levels out you can see across the well wooded Grève de Lecq valley to your right. On the far skyline you can see the former St Peter's Windmill.

• You pass the wall and gable of a ruin on the right and then the entrance to **Crabbè**
• **Rifle Range** on the left. Directly opposite this entrance is the winding path

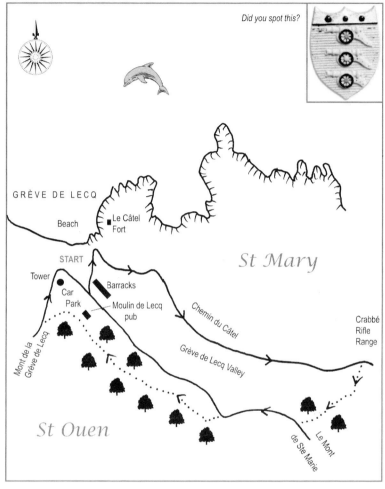

Did you spot this?

GRÈVE DE LECQ

Beach

Le Câtel
Fort

St Mary

START

Tower

Car
Park

Barracks

Moulin de Lecq
pub

Chemin du Câtel

Crabbé
Rifle
Range

Mont de la
Grève de Lecq

Grève de Lecq Valley

St Ouen

Le Mont
de Ste Marie

downhill (beware nettles and brambles in summer!) until you reach
the road, then turn right. This is **Mont de Ste. Marie**. Head down
here. Shortly beyond the right-hand bend you will see the start
of a footpath leading away to the left. Follow this until you reach
the stream in the valley bottom. Cross over by the stepping stones
and bear right to proceed down along the valley on the left bank.

You will eventually spot the buildings of the Moulin de Lecq pub below
to your right. Simply carry on until you reach the road. Bear right here
to reach the bay, the bus stop and car parks.

23 GREVE DE LECQ 2
via Mont de la Grève de Lecq & Mont Capel

This walk is most definitely off the beaten track along a succession of paths to which the public has access thanks to the generosity of a local landowner.

Distance:	2 kilometres	
Getting there:	Bus routes 7b, 9	
Parking:	There is usually ample space either in the car park surrounding the Martello Tower or in the one above the Romany Café.	
Refreshment:	Pubs include the Prince of Wales and the Moulin de Lecq (just uphill on the right along Le Mont de Ste. Marie); cafès are the Romany and, further along the sea wall to the left, Colleen's.	

- To begin the walk: Turn your back to the bay and bear right, past the **Prince of Wales Hotel** on your right, the car park surrounding the Martello Tower on your left.

- Look out for **Grève de Lecq Pumping Station** and Dead End sign on your right. Turn in here and proceed for a few yards, keeping to the left until you reach a wooden bridge across the laneside stream. Cross here to enter the meadow and follow the mown grass path to the left as it climbs steadily uphill, parallel to and beside the road.

- You pass the rear of a roofed drinking trough which faces the road. Exit the meadow by a 5-bar gate in the top right-hand corner to join the lane. Bear left to join the main road. Cross over, continue uphill and take the first on the left: **Rue du Mont Capel**, indicated as a cul de sac. This lane bears right at **Mont Capel Farm** and becomes a dirt track. Turn left over the step beside the 5-bar gate and follow the grassy, fenced track. On a clear day you will enjoy panoramic views across the sea towards the French coast.

- At a crossing of tracks turn right to reach the edge of the woods above Grève de Lecq Valley. Now bear left and very soon look out for a path leading off to the right and into the woods. Carry on until you reach a plank bench.

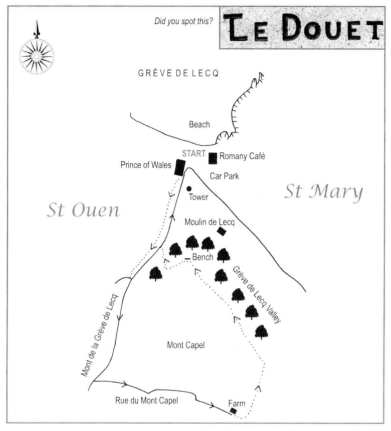

Did you spot this? **LE DOUET**

GRÈVE DE LECQ

Beach

START   Romany Café

Prince of Wales

Car Park

St Mary

Tower

St Ouen

Moulin de Lecq

Bench

Grève de Lecq Valley

Mont de la Grève de Lecq

Mont Capel

Rue du Mont Capel   Farm

This is a perfect spot to pause and absorb the scene. You are in an elevated position at the cusp of the two valleys which lead down to Grève de Lecq. You are also just below the tree line so your view towards the bay may be partly obscured by foliage in the summer. You will be reassured, however, by the sound of the sea washing up the beach, even if it is out of sight.

- Continue to follow the path but bearing right at points where there is
- a choice of ways. You begin to descend, at first by a flight of around 35
- steps. At its foot bear left and then right. Continue to descend the path,
- finally by a flight of 20 or so steps on the left in order to reach the road.
- Bear right to reach the bay and your starting point.

24 St OUEN
via Grève de Lecq Valley

This is a relatively challenging walk from St Ouen's parish centre via the woodland delights of Grève de Lecq Valley.

Distance:	4 kilometres
Getting there:	Bus routes 7b, 8, 9
Parking:	Public car park behind Parish Hall just off main road
Refreshment:	Farmers Inn pub; Snow Goose Tea Room

With your back to **St Ouen's Parish Hall** turn right and follow the main road. Pass the splendid new village green and turn right along **Rue de la Fosse au Bois**. Head through the dwellings of St Ouen's village and turn left at the T-junction ahead, then right at the main road. Look out for a narrow footpath on the left, about 200 metres ahead. This is Chemin du Prieur, though it is not signposted.

At the lane opposite **Spring Valley Farm** turn right. Looking left you can see the hump of Câtel de Lecq above Grève de Lecq.

Once past the buildings, look out for an unmade track to the left (evocatively known as known as Ruelle des Marineaux though, again, it is not signposted) – follow this as it begins to descend to reach a clump of trees, heralded by a rusty old 5-bar gate. Turn right here to follow a level path between a hedge to your right and a field to your left. You will see through the hedge on your right the grand house above aptly named Northdale.

Bear slightly to the right as the path becomes enclosed and head for the trees on the slopes ahead. First take the left fork, down valley, then a right fork to follow a lower path.

Follow the main path down a tributary valley which soon joins the main Grève de Lecq Valley – you will spot the road through the trees on the valley's far side. This is a mossy, ferny world of shadowy, ivy-clad trees, a complete contrast to the open uplands you have just left.

Continue to follow the main path, crossing a little side valley bearing a stream flowing left-right via a wooden causeway. After about 50 metres look out for a gap in the bank on the right – descend here to follow a lower path which runs parallel to the one you have been following.

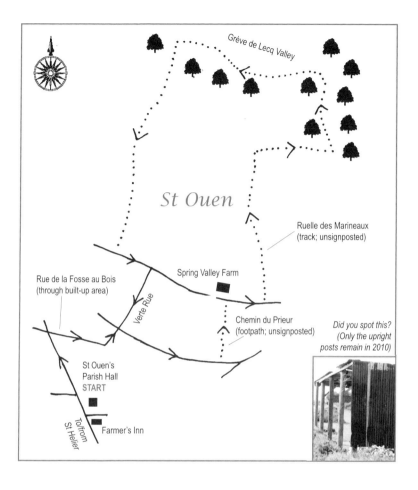

Grève de Lecq Valley

St Ouen

Ruelle des Marineaux
(track; unsignposted)

Rue de la Fosse au Bois
(through built-up area)

Spring Valley Farm

Verte Rue

Chemin du Prieur
(footpath; unsignposted)

Did you spot this?
(Only the upright
posts remain in 2010)

St Ouen's
Parish Hall
START

To/from
St Helier

Farmer's Inn

- This lower path crosses a stream flowing left to right, then embarks on
- a steady ascent. You bear left to emerge at a field. Now simply proceed
- along the track. Bear right to follow the hedged track, then very soon left
- between hedgebanks, then left beside a privet hedge on your right. Simply
- head straight on until you reach the lane where you turn left, then right
- via **Verte Rue** to reach your starting point in **St Ouen's village**.

25 PORTINFER
via Dolmen Hougue des Géonnais & Vinchelez

A surprising route which leads you through fields along footpaths and tracks to reach an ancient dolmen, then past manor houses and along Green Lanes. No steep slopes.

Distance:	2.5 kilometres
Getting there:	Bus routes 7b, 8
Parking:	There is a small car park near the crossroads, on the left along Route de Plémont.
Refreshment:	North Point Café/Restaurant at Portinfer crossroads; The Forge pub nearby.

To begin the walk: at **Portinfer crossroads**, with your back to North Point, bear right along **Route de Vinchelez** in an easterly direction. Very soon turn left along **Rue de la Croute** past **La Gabourellerie Farm** and into **Rue de la Gabourellerie**.

Just beyond the first field on your left look out for the entrance to a track on your left. Follow this as it reaches the end of this field and curves to the right where you follow the hedgebank on your right.

As you enter a second field you will enjoy an unimpeded view northwards over the sea and towards the rocks known as the Paternosters.

Beyond this field the way now forms a boundary path soon emphasised by stone walls on either side from which you will gain a view eastwards towards Sorel Point.

When you reach a junction of tracks you turn right. As houses come into view on your right look to your left for access to a feature known as **La Hougue des Géonnais**, an ancient passage grave and one of several in the island which occupies a typically splendid location. An explanatory notice here dates the grave at 6,000 years old. The dolmen can be found by bearing left as you enter the track.

Carry on along the lane until you reach its junction with **Route de Vinchelez**.

To the left is the entrance to **Le Manoir de Vinchelez de Bas** – Lower Vinchelez Manor.

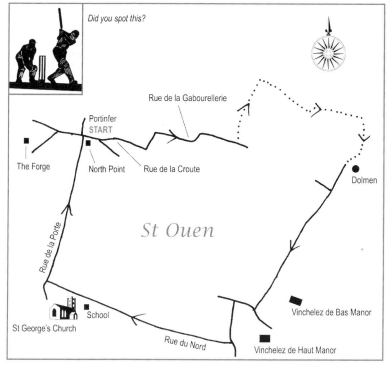

Note the stone steps set into the wall next to the entrance. If you bear left at this junction you will find a more ancient entrance to the Manor in the shape of an old gate with a keystone bearing the inscription carved in granite, ADC 1730. This old portal beside a lane overhung with branches was a favourite destination of early tourists and is a scene depicted on many an Edwardian postcard.

- Back at the junction with **Rue des Géonnais**, with your back to the lane from the Dolmen, bear right and sharp left. You will now pass **Vinchelez Manor de Haut** – Higher Vinchelez Manor. Now turn right into **Rue du Nord**.

- On your left you pass **Les Landes School** and **St George's Church**, with its distinctive saddle-back tower – not a parish church but a chapel of ease to St Ouen's. At the junction turn right into **Rue de la Porte** to reach **Portinfer crossroads** and the starting point.

26 GROSNEZ
via Les Landes S.S.I., footpaths & lanes

This walk takes you through the north-west corner of Jersey, perhaps the island's emptiest quarter, particularly Les Landes, open and windswept as it is.

Distance:	6 kilometres
Getting there:	Bus route
Parking:	There is a large public car park at Grosnez
Refreshment:	None

- From the car park at **Grosnez Castle**: with your back to the castle, head for the signpost in the ground to the right indicating the stretch ahead as **Les Landes Site of Special Scientific Interest**. Take the track to the left of the sign heading towards the perimeter fence of the racetrack. Follow this wide grit track flanked by heather and prostrate gorse, always with the white perimeter fence 50 metres or so to your left.

- The track draws closer to the fence where the racecourse curves away to the left. Carry on to reach a small parking area on your right and a low gate. Continue by the main track.

- At the T-junction you turn left. However, you may wish to explore the inviting looking path straight ahead. This describes a loop through the vegetation – mainly shoulder-high gorse providing good cover for pheasants. Very soon after starting on this path there is a bifurcation – an indicated footpath to the right and bridleway to the left. Either route takes you to a second low gate. Here turn back to complete the loop and return to the main track.

- On reaching the road, **Rue de la Mare**, cross over and follow the track between fields opposite. This is Rue de la Landelle, though there is no indication as such. When you reach the next road, facing a post box, turn right to approach the building ahead, **Les Landes Cottage**. Turn sharp left here to follow a boundary track between hedges. This is unmarked but goes by the name of Rue du Maresquet. You reach a dog-leg bend, after which the track reverts to a narrow path for a stretch. At a second dog leg there is a track leading off to the right. This is a diversion but if you head along here for about 50 metres you will find a rather mysterious pond shrouded by trees and backed by a rockface of what appears to be a former local quarry working.

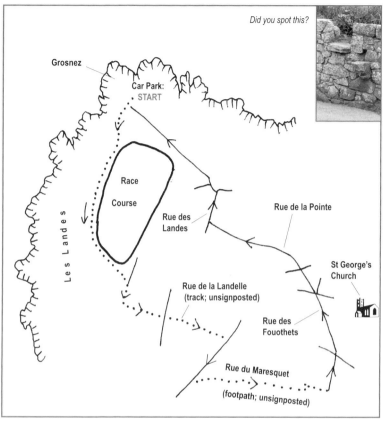

Did you spot this?

Grosnez
Car Park:
• START

Race
Course

Les Landes

Rue des
Landes

Rue de la Pointe

St George's
Church

Rue de la Landelle
(track; unsignposted)

Rue des
Fouothets

Rue du Maresquet

(footpath; unsignposted)

- Back on our route the path reverts once again to a track, then bears left and right to reach the road where you turn left.

- At the crossroads head straight on via **Rue des Fouothets**. You will spot the saddleback tower of St George's church across the fields to your right.

- At the next junction bear left, then immediately right via **La Nethe Rue**, then straight on at the next crossroads via **Rue de la Pointe**.

Note the drystone walls hereabouts – very much a feature of St Ouen's Parish.

- At the next T-junction turn right - you can see the racetrack to your left. Carry on until the road bears right - here locate the bus stop or, if you arrived by car, head left along the drive to return to Grosnez Castle.

27 JERSEY PEARL
via Grantez & St Ouen's Windmill

This is a longer walk, on a variety of footpaths, tracks and green lanes through the 'big country' of St Ouen's parish. And you can end with a stretch of coast path.

Distance:	6 kilometres
Getting there:	Bus route 12A
Parking:	There is a large public car park beside the lane almost opposite Jersey Pearl which leads down to the beach via Les Laveurs Slip.
Refreshment:	Café at Jersey Pearl. There is also a café at Jersey Woollen Mills a short distance along the main road which runs parallel to St Ouen's Bay.

- To begin the walk: With your back to the entrance to Jersey Pearl turn right. Follow the main road for a short distance and then turn right into **Chemin du Moulin**. Just beyond the first house on the left you will find the entrance to a footpath indicated by a footprint sign.

- Begin the gradual ascent until you reach a fork in the path. Don't bear left by what appears to be the main sandy path but head straight on and up by the grassy path.

- The way opens up and levels out at a kissing gate on the right. You can go through the gate here to reach the **Dolmen des Monts Grantez** in its walled enclosure across the field. Otherwise bear left across the little parking area and then right via an unmade track. A lane soon joins from the right but simply carry straight on. The rising valley to the left is Mont Pinel.

- At the T-junction bear right, not left along Le Vier Mont. When you reach the end of **Ruette de Grantez** you bear right once more, past **Chemin des Monts** which joins from the right.

- Further on, **Rue de Grantez** becomes **Rue du Couvent** and bears right. As you walk along here you will see St Ouen's Church to your left and the stump of St Ouen's Windmill to your right.

- At the junction with **Ville de l'Eglise** bear right along the stony track. Various other tracks lead off to right and left but you simply carry on along the main track ahead. You begin to descend, the view across St

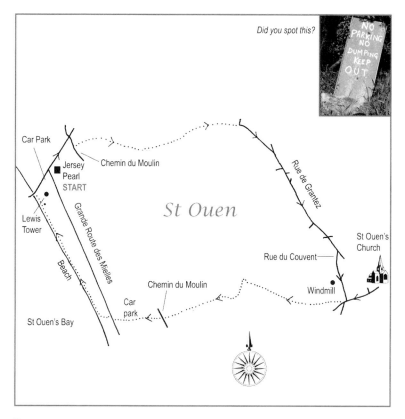

Did you spot this?

St Ouen

Car Park

Jersey
Pearl
START

Chemin du Moulin

Rue de Grantez

Lewis
Tower

Grande Route des Mielles

St Ouen's
Church

Rue du Couvent

Beach

Chemin du Moulin

Windmill

Car
park

St Ouen's Bay

Ouen's opening up with every step. Shortly after the track reverts to a narrow path, look out for a path branching off to the left. Follow this path which becomes increasingly rough as it descends across outcrops of bedrock. When you encounter a fork, bear left. The path levels out and once again becomes a track between fields.

At the road cross over and follow the signposted footpath opposite. Once beyond the grassed-over sand dunes you bear right to a little car park where there is a board featuring this area, **La Mielle de Morville**, and its History, Fauna and Flora.

Carry on seaward until you reach the road. Cross over and bear right to complete the walk. You have the choice of walking along the path beside the road or heading along the sea wall. If the latter then you will leave the sea wall to pass to the right of the **Channel Island Military Museum** and **Lewis Tower** before reaching the car park and **Jersey Pearl**.

28 St OUEN'S BAY

via Big Vern's, Val de la Mare Reservoir & Mont Rossignol

A longish but varied route exploring the wide open spaces of St Ouen's, with some great views en route. Much of the walk is off-road or via footpaths and quiet lanes.

Distance:	5.5 kilometres
Getting there:	Bus route 12A
Parking:	L'Ouzière car park
Refreshment:	Big Vern's or Watersplash en route

- To begin the walk: With your back to **L'Ouzière car park** and **Big Vern's Diner** and facing the sea, turn left in a southerly direction by the coast path.

- Once past the Watersplash bear left to follow the path beside the road. Cross over and take the first lane on the left, **Route de la Marette**. Pass **Les Mielles Activity Centre** and negotiate a dog-leg bend.

- Here you turn right along **Route du Moulin**. You will see the dam containing Val de la Mare Reservoir to your left. Turn off the lane here and follow the track which heads towards the dam's left-hand corner. Now make your way up the footpath beside the noticeboard.

- At the top of this path you turn right to follow the perimeter of the reservoir. However, our route entails bearing left here, still climbing up a track.

This affords wide views over St Ouen's Bay and back over the Reservoir – a more attractive prospect than perhaps it sounds, particularly when the reservoir is full.

- The track curves to the right and forks - take the left fork to reach the road; this is **Mont Rossignol**, one of several roads which descend to St Ouen's Bay. Bear right and soon turn left into **Rue de la Campagne**.

- Before you reach the first house ahead look out for the start of a track on your left. Head down here. At a fork bear left by the main track to reach a 5-bar gate. Here you enter a bramble-topped promontory with some wide, mown paths. Keep bearing left (but don't descend to the road) and the path will carry you in a loop, clockwise fashion, until you arrive at a second gate just to the left of the one you passed through earlier.

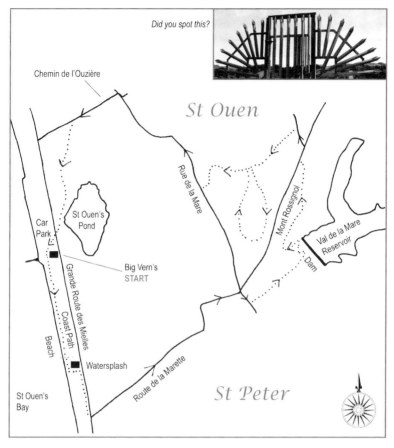

- Keep bearing left and begin to descend – I've been told that this is the old coffin path along which the dead were transported from the western reaches of St Ouen's to the parish church.

- Keep bearing left until you emerge at the property known as **Les Crecerelles** on the right. Follow the track until you drop down onto **Rue de la Mare**. Turn right, enjoying the view across St Ouen's Pond towards the sea, and turn left into **Chemin de l'Ouzière**.

- Look out for the signpost indicating access to **Le Noir Pré Orchid Field** on the left. Just past here, at the low-slung bar, bear left. Follow the beaten path diagonally across this open space towards **Big Vern's** and **L'Ouzière car park** – doing so you will be walking off-road to complete the route.

29 St PETER
via Airport & Rue du Val de la Mare du Sud

If you like aeroplanes you will enjoy the first stretch of this route as it follows the airport's northern perimeter. Further on the walk affords some tremendous views as it descends Jubilee Hill and ascends again on the far side of the valley. The route is largely off-road apart from, unavoidably, one or two short sections.

Distance:	5 kilometers
Getting there:	Bus route no. 9 & 15 (sometimes)
Parking:	Public car park behind St Peter's Parish Hall
Refreshment:	Pubs and cafés in St Peter's Village

* From the car park head along **Petite Rue des Fosses** beside the church wall. Turn right at the end along **Rue du Presbytère**, then left at the main road. Pass **St Peter's School** to your left and the parish's **Millennium Stone.**

* Bear left here along **Route de l'Hermité** then right to follow the airport perimeter. This lane rejoins **Mont du Jubilé** at the parish's Millennium Cross. In order to avoid walking on the road you can climb up on to the grassy bank beside the fence. After 100 metres or so turn left into **Rue du Mont au Guet**, descend by the wooden steps, then bear right along the grit track to follow the airport's perimeter fence. There is plenty of open space between you and the road.

As you walk on the view gradually widens towards St Ouen's Bay. To the right, northwards, you can see the spire of St Ouen's Church and the stump of its former windmill.

* When you reach a bench you must divert to the right but carry on via the beaten path as it gradually descends and bears to the left via a kissing gate beside a 5-bar gate to reach a lane. The left-hand way, uphill, is a dead end and leads to **Elm Farm**.

* Turn right along **Rue du Val de la Mare du Sud**. It is advisable to cross over to negotiate the right-hand curve ahead; note the abreuvoir at the roadside.

* Bear right at the busier road ahead, then shortly left into **Route du Moulin**.

* Head up the concrete ramp next to the entrance to Rue du Mont de la

Did you spot this?

Rue de la Presse

Chemin du Mont de la Mare

St Peter's Church

Ville du Bocage

School

Parish Hall

Rue de l'Hermite

Mont du Jubilée

Rue du Mont du Guet

Airport runway

Mare. This gives access to a car park for Bethesda Chapel and associated buildings. At the top of the ramp bear right by the beaten path along the field edge. At the top you will see the exit onto the lane – turn left here to follow the path which soon curves to the right to resume an uphill course in an easterly direction.

This narrow path exits on to a track. Continue in the same general direction to reach the signpost for '**Eagles Rock**', then carry straight on. To your left you will see down towards Val de la Mare Reservoir and to your right a house with an impressive pair of Dutch gables.

You reach the end of **Les Monts** to carry on along **Rue de la Presse**. At the crossroads you reach the built up area of St Peter's Village to enter **Ville du Bocage**, a large estate built in the 1970s which, pleasingly, retains a number of green open spaces.

Head on towards the spire of **St Peter's Church**. When the road turns left you may head along the cul de sac to the right where you will find a path between houses which leads directly to the main road back to the church and St Peter's **Parish Hall**.

30 LA PULENTE
via L'Oeillere & Petit Port

This short walk, entirely off-road, takes you around and over the promontory at the southern end of St Ouen's Bay. The final climb offers splendid views in every direction.

Distance:	1.5 kilometres	
Getting there:	Bus route 12a	
Parking:	There is limited parking at the head of the slipway at La Pulente. Alternatively there is a large car park on the right of the road beside the bay.	
Refreshment:	La Pulente pub.	

● To begin the walk: Facing **La Pulente pub** at the head of the slipway turn
● right along the narrow path beside the seaward side of the road.

● As you reach the hillside ahead you will see a flight of steps leading
● upwards. Ignore these (we will make their descent on the return leg of
● the walk) but bear right to follow the level path around the headland
● called L'Oeillere.

This path affords long views across St Ouen's Bay towards La Rocco Tower, the restored Martello Tower on a rocky outcrop offshore and to Le Pinacle, the distinctively upright rock which punctuates the northern reach of the bay.

You also pass extensive German fortifications built during the years of Occupation.

● The path negotiates the end of the promontory and the view changes
● accordingly.

Corbière Lighthouse can be seen in a west-south-west direction and, nearer to hand, the rocky inlet know as Petit Port, complete with its elegantly curved slipway.

● Now branch right by the stepped path to descend to the slipway, then left
● at the footprint sign, just before the recently built **Sea Crest** apartment
● block.

● As the path curves to the left you reach a stile on the right. This rightward
● course leads you to a stream and eventually to the main road. However,

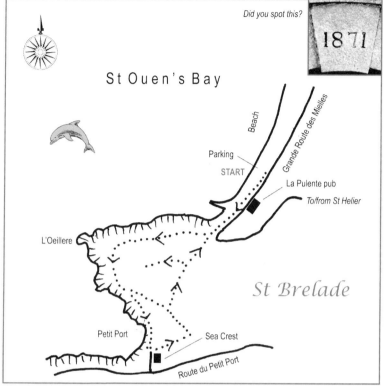

Did you spot this?

St Ouen's Bay

Beach

Grande Route des Mielles

Parking

START

La Pulente pub

To/from St Helier

L'Oeillere

St Brelade

Petit Port

Sea Crest

Route du Petit Port

- our route continues along the main path as it branches right to climb the hill.

- You reach a junction of paths at the summit.

Before you descend the far side it is well worth taking the path to the left to reach the 163 feet summit of L'Oeillere which provides panoramic views in all directions. The next land mass in a westerly direction is Newfoundland, some three thousand miles away.

There is a prehistoric passage grave in the vicinity but more in evidence are yet more German fortifications.

- Back at the junction of paths turn left to begin the descent and return to **La Pulente.**

31 St BRELADE 1
via La Moye & Les Creux Country Park

This walk is almost all off-road. The route includes part of the coast path from St Brelade's to Beauport and stretches within the recently created Les Creux Country Park. Other than a steep ascent and descent at the start and finish, the route is on the level.

Distance:	2.5 - 3.5 kilometres
Getting there:	Bus route 14
Parking:	Car parks in the bay to the landward side
Refreshment:	Cafés, bars and the Pizza Express Restaurant in St Brelade's Bay

To begin the walk: Head towards the **Parish Church** which nestles above the sea wall in the west corner of St Brelade's Bay. With your back to the lych gate facing the Church Hall bear left, uphill, until you reach the steps at the indicated start of the path to Beauport. Simply follow the way as it ascends the hillside and begins to level out.

Where the path forks, take the right fork. Cross the metalled track and continue in the same direction by the grassy path opposite, signposted to **Mont ès Croix**.

On reaching a T-junction of paths turn left. At the junction of ways turn right and head straight on to reach the lane just opposite the bungalow. Turn left along the lane. You soon reach the start of a recently created footpath opposite **Verte Rue**; this forms a link with La Moye School via Les Creux Country Park. You may prefer to follow this, Route 1, as an alternative way which avoids a stretch of main road. It joins up with the longer route at point X on sketch map. Route 2 includes a pleasant boundary track between hedges.

For Route 2 carry on, passing a post box on the right. At the minor junction ahead you turn right along an unmade track between fields. When you reach the road you can see the name **Oak Lane** raised in the concrete rendering at the side of the dwelling on your right.

Turn right here with care. You can cross over towards **La Moye Garage** where there is a pavement for a short distance. However, it is not very

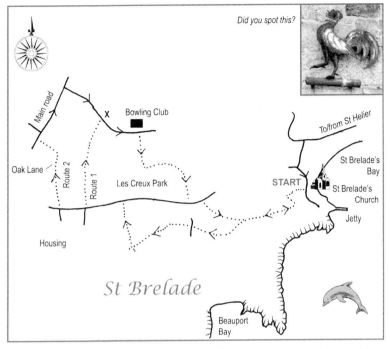

far to the next stage of the walk which involves turning right, off the road, into **Les Creux Country Park**.

Once through the impressive entrance bear left to follow a path which runs parallel to the drive. When you reach the **Bowls Clubhouse** turn right along the path beside the edge of the field signposted to St Brelade's Bay & Le Beau Port. Follow this grit path as it bears left to follow the field boundary with the hedgerow on your right. Cross the footbridge and bear left. Now simply follow the winding path as it heads beside the boundary wall of La Moye House and eventually follows a course parallel to the entrance drive to the house.

On reaching the lane turn left. Pass the turn-off on the right to Beauport and soon look out for a sign on the right indicating an off-road route back to **St Brelade's Church**. Head along here and enjoy the views across St Brelade's Bay towards the promontories reaching up to Portelet Common. When you reach a metal gate bear right to rejoin the coast path which we followed at the start of the walk. Retrace your steps back down to the lane near the church.

32 St BRELADE 2

*via Churchill Memorial Park, Quennevais, Railway Walk &
Jersey's longest staircase*

Although mainly off-road, this walk passes through the built-up centre
of Quennevais, Jersey's largest commercial centre outside St Helier.
Nevertheless, this shortish route offers much variety.

Distance:	5 kilometres
Getting there:	Bus route 14
Parking:	Woodford car park at the west end of the bay
Refreshment:	Cafés, bars and the Pizza Express Restaurant in St Brelade's Bay; en route: Horse and Hound pub and cafés in Quennevais, Lavender Farm Restaurant

- With your back to the entrance to **Woodford Car Park** turn left towards
the entrance to **Churchill Memorial Park**. Go past the fountain on your
left then bear left via the main path - you will see the waterfall to your
right. Now simply follow the main path as it begins to climb the slope,
at first gently but soon quite steeply.

- You eventually reach the top entrance/exit. Walk straight ahead along
the drive which serves the dwellings here until you reach the main road.
Cross over to the pavement and bear right. You soon reach the crossroads
with the large **Checkers Supermarket** on your left and a branch of **Marks
& Spencer** on the opposite corner.

- Cross the road and continue in the same direction, then take the crossing
towards the **Post Office/Coop Locale** store on the far side. Bear left to
cross **Rue du Pont Marquet**, head past the shopping precinct until you
reach Don Bridge. If you miss the stone wall on either side of the road,
look out for the bus shelter on the far side which is clearly indicated as
the stop known as **Don Bridge**. Bear right down the slope behind the bus
stop here to join the **Railway Walk**. Cross a minor road.

- Look out for a **pond** on your right. Just past this the Walk meets a main
road, **Rue du Pont Marquet**. Don't cross the road but look out for the
start of a footpath on the right, just beside the bins. Head along this
shady way which runs parallel with the road on your left.

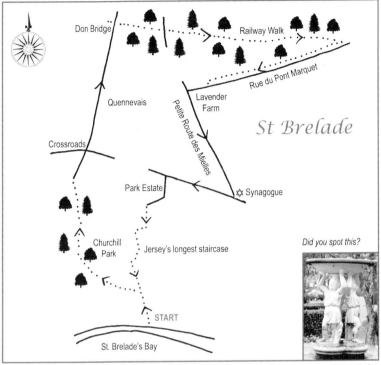

Did you spot this?

You emerge from the trees opposite **Hollycroft House** – head straight on by the path until you reach the fields of the **Lavender Farm**. Again, simply head on until you reach a stile directly opposite the entrance to the Farm.

Cross the road, bear right, and soon take the first on the left, again passing lavender fields. There is no pavement here but this lane – **Petite Route des Mielles** - is generally quiet. When you reach the main road cross over and turn right, then left into **Park Estate**. Keep bearing right – note the signpost indicating '**Footpath to St Brelade's Bay**'. Immediately past the house '**South View**' you will find the start of the '**Steps to St Brelade's Bay**'. Indeed, the last time I counted them, there were 276! This must be the island's longest staircase and the reason why this route turns clockwise rather than the other way round.

The foot of the steps drops you into **Churchill Memorial Park** where you retrace your steps back to the car park/bus stop.

33 St AUBIN 1

via La Haule, High Street, Market Hill & The Boulevard

This pleasant walk leads you through built-up St Aubin which must rate as one of the most picturesque and interesting parts of Jersey's built environment. There is an optional off-road walk via the wooded hillside just beyond the entrance to Mont de la Rocque.

Distance:	2 kilometres	
Getting there:	Bus routes 12, 12a, 14, 15	
Parking:	There is a public car park behind the Parish Hall and limited opportunities for on street parking beside the Harbour and along the main road.	
Refreshment:	A wide range of places available, from pubs to restaurants and cafés and a variety of cuisines.	

- From the road junction at the centre of St Aubin, walk past St Brelade's Parish Room, **'Salle Paroisialle de Saint Brelade'**, eastwards along the pavement.

Unusually, this parish room is nowhere near the parish church which is tucked into the far corner of St Brelade's Bay, a long way from here.

- Head along the footpath beside the sea wall. You pass the **Sacred Heart Catholic Church** on the far side beyond which rises a steep bank topped with a row of buildings.

- At the road junction turn left up **Mont au Roux**, past **La Haule Manor Hotel** and **Lucas Bros Farm Shop**. A little further uphill a Footpath sign on the right indicates the start (and finish) of a loop which explores the wooded hillside here and makes a leafy if energetic addition to this mainly urban walk.

- To continue the main route: Turn left into **Mont de la Rocque**. Where the road forks, take the left-hand route indicated as **Rue du Crocquet**, or **High Street**. You will now be presented with an elevated view towards St Aubin's Fort and beyond. Carry on past **La Tour Hotel** with its classically-styled pilasters and many fine and attractive old houses, some with their original wooden shutters. The street becomes cobbled as it slopes down to reach the main road. Cross the main road but notice, to the right, the start of the Railway Walk to Corbière.

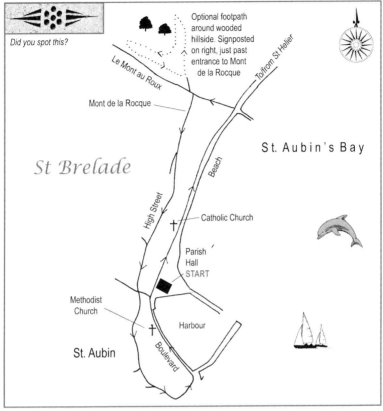

Did you spot this?

Optional footpath around wooded hillside. Signposted on right, just past entrance to Mont de la Rocque

Le Mont au Roux

Mont de la Rocque

Toɪfrom St Helier

St. Aubin's Bay

St Brelade

Beach

High Street

Catholic Church

Parish Hall
START

Methodist Church

Harbour

St. Aubin

Boulevard

Continue the walk by ascending **Rue au Moestre**, or **Market Hill**. Notice the staircase on the left which drops down to Quai Bisson. Carry on past the foot of **Mont Arthur**, the steep lane on your right, then bear left down **Mont es Tours**. You pass the entrance to the **Somerville Hotel** and eventually drop down via **Mont du Boulevard** to the Harbour.

The **Channel Islands Yacht Club** is on your right and the **Old Court House** on your left. As you make your way beside the harbour to the main road you will pass a succession of eating places, in addition to some more attractive old houses, mostly set well back from the road, as well as a couple of Boat Yards, the Methodist Church and the Harbour Gallery which is well worth a visit. Finally, as you reach the main road, notice the **NatWest bank** which was formerly a market hall, with an indication of a former collection box with its lettering 'Souvenez-vous des Pauvres'.

34 St AUBIN 2

via Mont de la Rocque, Mont Nicolle, Mont Gras d'Eau,
Ouaisné Common & Mont du Ouaisné

This is a relatively long walk around the parish of St Brelade. There are four 'Monts' en route with steady climbs up three of them. The route is varied and includes quiet lanes, coastal path, a circuit of Ouaisné Common and plenty of good views.

Distance:	7 kilometres 👢 👢
Getting there:	Bus routes 12, 12a, 14, 15
Parking:	There is a public car park behind the Parish Hall and limited opportunities for on street parking beside the Harbour and along the main road.
Refreshment:	A wide range of pubs, restaurants and cafés in St Aubin from offering a variety of cuisines. There are also opportunities en route, including the Wayside Café in St Brelade's Bay and the Old Smugglers Inn at Ouaisné.

To begin the walk: With your back to the **Parish Hall**, facing the Harbour, bear right to cross the road and head up **Charing Cross**. Soon turn right at the **Trafalgar** pub. This is **High Street**. You pass many attractive old houses to reach an open aspect on the right overlooking St Aubin's Fort and Bay. Immediately past here look out for the staircase which climbs the wall on the left. Head up here and turn left at the top.

Follow the road as it bears right at **Ste Cecilia** – a newly built block of flats which effectively blocks the view. You reach a T-junction where you turn left. The lane twists and turns and passes the entrance to the house called **Le Bocage** which gives its name to the road. **Rue du Bocage** ends at a T-junction where you turn left. At the next junction (not as far as the main road) turn sharp right.

Descend a little and note the steps to the left reaching up to the Railway Walk. Pass beneath the former railway bridge and cross the stream. Now you begin ascending **Mont Nicolle** via the hairpin bend at the house called **Sous les Bois**.

You reach the top of **Mont Nicolle** at the main road; turn right, cross the road at the bus stop and descend **Mont Gras d'Eau** to **St Brelade's Bay**. Cross the road and head towards the beach. Turn left at the Wayside Café

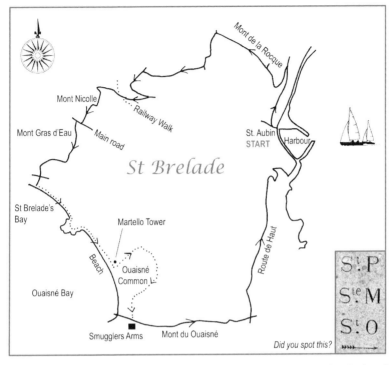

St Brelade

Did you spot this?

and walk along the path above the sea wall. At the headland ahead climb the steps. Bear right and immediately left up the flight of steps. Simply follow the main which soon descends to reach the sea wall above Ouaisné. Follow the path which runs a few metres on the landward side of the wall.

Just past the **Martello Tower**, at the signpost naming this Ouaisné Common, turn left and follow the footpath through the gorse, bracken and heather. The way curves to the right below the villas on the hillside above and eventually exits at a track where you turn right. This will take you to top of the car park at Ouaisné. Carry on to reach the road at **The Old Smugglers Inn**. Turn left uphill; this is **Mont du Ouaisné**.

The lane eventually levels out at a crossroads. Here you turn left along **Route de Noirmont**. Bear right along **Route de Haut** which eventually descends through a series of hairpin bends, past the guarded entrances to some grand residences to end at **Mont es Tours**. Here bear right past the entrance to **Somerville Hotel** and proceed down **Mont du Boulevard** to **St Aubin's Harbour** and your starting point.

---

35 BEAUMONT
via Rue du Craslin, Le Drédillet & Ruelle as Ruaux

This shortish walk makes use of a few stretches of footpath but is otherwise on back roads, with two busy thoroughfares to cross.

Distance:	4 kilometres 👢👢
Getting there:	Bus routes 9, 12, 12a, 14, 15
Parking:	Limited public parking at Gunsite Café; larger car parks before and after Beaumont junction
Refreshment:	Pubs Foresters Arms, The Goose at Beaumont. En route: Bistro Soleil, Gunsite Café,

From the busy junction at The Goose pub, make your way up **Beaumont Hill**, keeping to the pavement on the right.

Leave the road by turning right below Les Marais Cottages at the **Coop**. Head through the car park for **Total Sport** where you will find the start of a footpath in the left-hand corner of the car park. Follow the path beside the stream on your left until you reach a lane.

Turn left to reach **Rue du Craslin**. Bear right past **Le Drédillet** and carry on through a right and left-hand turn. Turn left up **Mont de Grupieaux**, a designated Green Lane. When you reach the house called **Le Vioge**, bear to the left of the house and make for the track signposted **Ruette à la Vioge: Pedestrians Only**. This is a steady climb – be sure to look left as you progress for far-reaching views over Beaumont and St Aubin's Bay.

At the summit bear left, past **Wheatland**s and take the first left: **Rue des Lauriers**. Turn left at the T-junction; this is Le Vieux Beaumont, the old road between Beaumont and St Peter and, as such, not much used by through traffic. You begin to descend and the road takes a sharp turn rightwards; at this point look out for the entrance to a path signposted **Le Drédillet: Pedestrians Only**. Head down here turning first right, then left, past some attractive old houses, until you rejoin Rue du Craslin. Turn right and carry on until you reach the main road.

Cross over to reach the grassy area distinguished by a cannon dating from the reign of Edward VI.

Cross the main road, with care, and make for the lane opposite, **Ruelle es Ruaux**. Once past the blocks of flats the lane bears to the left beside

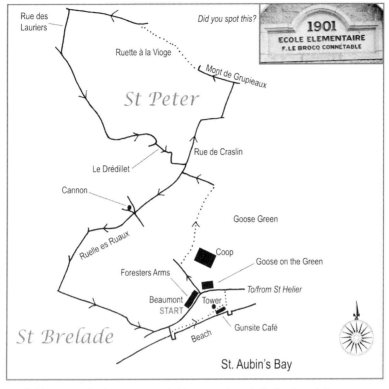

fields to reach the coast road. Here you turn left. Look out for a gap on
the right which leads to the beach and coast path. Cross over.

You will notice a tablet set in the wall on the right commemorating the
building of La Route de la Haule, as the coast road between here and
St Aubin is known. The tablet also informs that La Route de la Haule is
within the Parish of St Brelade, the stream which we have followed from
the point where La Ruelle es Ruaux swung left marks the boundary of
St Peter and St Brelade.

- Bear left along the coast path, past the Bistro Soleil, a fine Martello Tower
- and the Gunsite Café, so named because it is housed in a converted World
- War 2 concrete bunker. Bear left immediately past the café to join the
- road where you turn left to reach Beaumont junction and its two pubs.

36 BEAUMONT
via Promenade, Coronation Park & Rue de Haut

This is an easy but varied walk which takes in a stretch along the sea wall overlooking St Aubin's Bay, a stroll through the delightful Coronation Park. Following this, a quiet and slightly elevated walk a little inland offers a different view across Jersey's southerly bay. Ruelle Corbel, an all too short boundary path leads us across the main road and around the perimeter of the recently built La Providence estate, then via some newly laid paths back to our starting point.

Distance:	3 kilometres
Getting there:	Bus routes 9, 12, 12a, 14, 15
Parking:	Car park between road and promenade just before Gunsite Café and Beaumont junction
Refreshment:	Gunsite Café and pubs at Beaumont junction; En route: Cafe in Coronation Park

- From the bus stop and car park make for the promenade beside St Aubin's Bay and walk in an easterly direction, i.e. towards town.

- Carry on for around one kilometre. Look out for a pathside shelter. The trees opposite signal the site of **Coronation Park**. Cross Victoria Avenue with care – there is a refuge between the carriageways and enter the park by the main gate. Follow the path to the round pond, then on to the pavilion, then left.

You will pass a stone which records that the site was gifted to the island and a park created to commemorate the Coronation of King George VI in 1937.

- You will see a paddling pool to your left and a large children's playground on your right – there is also a café here which may or may not be open. You soon reach the road; now cross over.

- Bear right towards town then, at the busy junction ahead, turn sharp left into **Rue de Haut**. This is a one-way street and not usually very busy. There is a pavement all the way. The way rises slightly so that, once past the houses to your left, the view opens up across some remaining green fields towards the crescent of St Aubin's Bay.

- As the road curves to the left beside the grounds of Bel Royal Primary School on the left and the **Little Grove** Nursing Home on the right, carry straight on in the same direction along a footpath signposted as **Ruelle Corbel**.

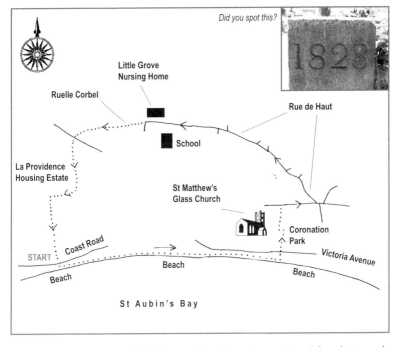

Did you spot this?

Ruelle Corbel

Little Grove
Nursing Home

Rue de Haut

School

La Providence
Housing Estate

St Matthew's
Glass Church

Coronation
Park

START   Coast Road

Beach

Beach

Victoria Avenue

Beach

St Aubin's Bay

This has the pleasant feel of an ancient boundary path as it heads towards the main road leading to the right towards St Peter's Valley. Bear left and carefully cross the road towards the large new estate of houses known as **La Providence**. Go through the main entrance and head towards the left of the houses, soon reaching a perimeter grit path.

Follow this path beside the neat little houses. Just beyond No. 97 you reach an arch on the right; this leads to a thoroughfare which bisects the estate. Turn left here to follow a recently created path across the low-lying field – so low-lying that there is usually standing water at one point beside the path. This area has been planted with trees and, in years to come, will no doubt provide a haven for wildlife. Providing, of course, that it does not become covered with more houses in the meantime.

The path makes its way between houses to lead you back to the coast road. Turn right towards the bus stop or use the crossing ahead to return to the car park.

THE COUNTRY CODE

Guard against all risk of fire
Fasten all gates
Keep dogs under proper control
Keep to the paths across farm land
Avoid damaging fences, hedges and walls
Leave no litter
Safeguard water supplies
Protect wild life, wild plants and trees
Go carefully on country roads
Respect the life of the countryside

To these ten points, a local landowner, who generously allows the public to use paths through his land, has asked that an eleventh rule should be added, namely, that dog owners should clear up the mess their pets produce!

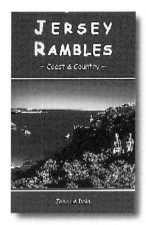
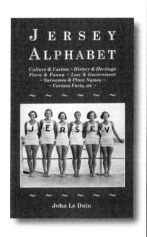

The 'JOURNEY JERSEY' trilogy by Robin Pittman

Perfect reads for the armchair rambler. Join Robin Pittman as he traverses his island home, first round Jersey's coast, then from side to side across the Island, and finally along the streets of St Helier. Meet the host of characters whom he encounters along the way as they talk about their lives. A fascinating picture of Jersey and its inhabitants in the early twenty-first century and an invaluable record for the future.

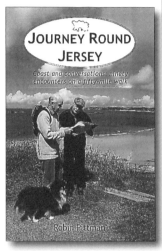

JOURNEY ROUND JERSEY
Coast and conversations: Ninety encounters on a fity-mile walk
Ilustrations by Jefferson Randles
ISBN 1 903341 28 0; 176 pages; £7.95
Published 2005, reprinted 2009

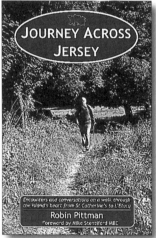

JOURNEY ACROSS JERSEY
Encounters and conversations on a walk through the Island's heart from St Catherine's to L'Etacq
Illustrations by Jefferson Randles
Foreword by Mike Stentiford MBE
ISBN 978-1-903341-44-5; 96 pages; £5.95
Published 2007

JOURNEY ROUND St HELIER
Six strolls discovering people and places in the town at the centre of Jersey's affairs
Illustrations by David Barton
Foreword by Simon Crowcroft, Connétable of St Helier
ISBN 978-1-906641-12-2; 160 pages; £7.95
Published 2009

More books on the Channel Islands from Seaflower:

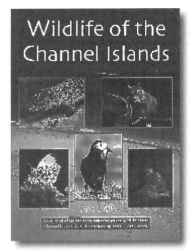

WILDLIFE OF THE CHANNEL ISLANDS
by Sue Daly
A beautiful and informative book featuring some 240 superb photographs in full-colour.
ISBN 1 903341 24 8; 221 pages; £14.95

GUERNSEY COUNTRY DIARY: *Through the Natural Year* with Nigel Jee
Informative, amusing and altogether delightful account of the natural year in Guernsey.
ISBN 0 948578 90 4; 128 pages; £4.95

JERSEY WEATHER AND TIDES
by Peter Manton
Jersey's weather sets records in the UK and its tides are some of the world's biggest. Learn more from this book.
ISBN 0 948578 75 0; 96 pages; £5.95

JERSEY WITCHES, GHOSTS & TRADITIONS
by Sonia Hillsdon
New edition of a book first published twenty years ago.
ISBN 1 903341 13 2; 160 pages; £6.50

JERSEY: NOT QUITE BRITISH:
The Rural History of a Singular People
by David Le Feuvre
Absorbing account of Jersey's rural heritage.
ISBN 1 903341 27 2; 160 pages; £6.95

THE JERSEY LILY:
The Life and Times of Lillie Langtry
by Sonia Hillsdon
Our second bestselling title.
ISBN 0 948578 55 6; 128 pages; £5.95

JERSEY HORSES FROM THE PAST
by John Jean
Pictorial presentation of the vital role our four-legged friends once played.
ISBN 0 903341 01 9; 96 pages; £4.95

JERSEY IN LONDON
by Brian Ahier Read
Story of the Jersey Society in London, which played a vital role during the war years.
ISBN 0 948578 64 5; 192 pages; £6.95

EXOTIC GARDEN PLANTS IN THE CHANNEL ISLANDS
by Janine Le Pivert
ISBN 978-903341-40-7; 129 pages; £9.95

WILD ISLAND: Jersey Nature Diary
by Peter Double
The natural year in Jersey, profusely and beautifully illustrated.
ISBN 0 948578 77 7; 120 pages; £7.95

A FARMER'S VACATION IN 1873
Jersey - Guernsey - Sark
by George E Waring Jnr.
ISBN 978-1-903341-43-8; 76 pages; £5.00

Our two bestselling Channel Islands cookbooks ~

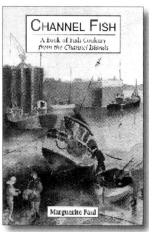

CHANNEL FISH: *A Book of Fish Cookery from the Channel Islands* by Marguerite Paul.
Our bestselling fish cookery book.
ISBN 0 903341 10 8; 24 pages; £9.95

ISLAND KITCHEN: *A Book of Seasonal Cookery from the Channel Islands* by Marguerite Paul
Follow-up to 'Channel Fish', featuring seasonal produce, local and not-so-local recipes.
ISBN 0 903341 18 3; 192 pages; £9.95

Books on Sark ~

ISLAND DESTINY: *A true story of love and war in the Channel Island of Sark* by Richard Le Tissier
'One of the most remarkable stories of the German Occupation'– *Jersey Evening Post*
ISBN 1-903341-36-1; 160 pages; £6.95

MINED WHERE YOU WALK: *The German Occupation of Sark, 1940-45* by Richard Le Tissier
ISBN 978-1-906641-00-9; 144 pages; £6.95

LIFE ON SARK; *Through the year with Jennifer Cochrane*
ISBN 1-903341-25-6; 128 pages; £5.95